THE WORLD OF
LOVEBIRDS

H-1092

© **Copyright 1990 by T.F.H. Publications, Inc.**

Distributed in the UNITED STATES by T.F.H. Publications, Inc., One T.F.H. Plaza, Neptune City, NJ 07753; in CANADA to the Pet Trade by H & L Pet Supplies Inc., 27 Kingston Crescent, Kitchener, Ontario N2B 2T6; Rolf C. Hagen Ltd., 3225 Sartelon Street, Montreal 382 Quebec; in CANADA to the Book Trade by Macmillan of Canada (A Division of Canada Publishing Corporation), 164 Commander Boulevard, Agincourt, Ontario M1S 3C7; in ENGLAND by T.F.H. Publications Limited, Cliveden House/Priors Way/Bray, Maidenhead, Berkshire SL6 2HP, England; in AUSTRALIA AND THE SOUTH PACIFIC by T.F.H. (Australia) Pty. Ltd., Box 149, Brookvale 2100 N.S.W., Australia; in NEW ZEALAND by Ross Haines & Son, Ltd., 82 D Elizabeth Knox Place, Panmure, Auckland, New Zealand; in the PHILIPPINES by Bio-Research, 5 Lippay Street, San Lorenzo Village, Makati Rizal; in SOUTH AFRICA by Multipet Pty. Ltd., Box 235, New Germany, South Africa 3620. Published by T.F.H. Publications, Inc. Manufactured in the United States of America by T.F.H. Publications, Inc.

THE WORLD OF
LOVEBIRDS

Jürgen Brockmann
and
Werner Lantermann

J.R.Quinn

Translated by WILLIAM CHARLTON

Note to the English-language Edition

In an effort to make lovebird genetics easier to understand, in this edition the *names* of the lovebird color varieties and of the genetic factors responsible for them are capitalized; this helps to distinguish references to the color variety named *Green* from instances where the word *green* is used merely to describe coloration. The names here given to the varieties necessarily reflect the usage of the German edition, while the Appendix lists those few instances in which the names used here differ from those that have more currency in English-speaking countries.

The genetic factors have been named and symbolized according to the traits that they produce. In most cases it has been possible to use the initial of the name as the letter-symbol for the factor. For example: the variety Blue (or Pastel-blue) is the product of the Blue factor, symbolized as *b*. Following the conventions of geneticists, the letter is lower-cased because the Blue factor is recessive. A capital-letter symbol signifies dominant or intermediate inheritance.

For simplicity, only the factors pertinent to the discussion at hand are listed when the genotype is symbolized. It would be impossibly cumbersome to include each time the symbols of all the factors present; for example, if all the traits given symbols in this book were included, the genotype of the male wild-colored Peach-faced Lovebird would be written *BdBdYYppEEFFQQwwooICIC*.

Contents

Preface to the Second Edition

When a second edition of our book on lovebirds is necessary barely three years after the appearance of the first printing, it is evident that these small African parrots are apparently enjoying unchanged or even increasing popularity among bird keepers.

Knowledge about five of the six species of lovebirds (the exception is the Black-collared Lovebird, which, to the best of our knowledge, is not represented in any European collection) has in the meantime become very extensive—in contrast to other species of parrots—especially since they have repeatedly been the subject of biological, ethological, and lately even ecological research.

We have dealt with the color varieties and have explained their inheritance in particular detail. If we offer a greatly expanded book—compared to the first edition—this is mostly because new research findings about the varieties have been incorporated into the second part of the book.

The literature treating this genus of small parrots has also increased greatly, so that we have had to almost double the original bibliography. For this we must thank, not least, the members of the Arbeitsgemeinschaft Agaporniden (AGA, 'lovebird workshop'), as they have published many fundamental contributions in a monthly newsletter since the founding of the Interessengemeinschaft ('specialty association') in 1981.

Our gratitude also goes to veterinarian Dr. Uta Ebert of Hannover for reviewing the chapter on illnesses; to Dr. Joachim Steinbacher of the Senckenberg Institute in Frankfurt for his expert advice; and to Pastor Werner Wiching of Ahaus for his practical help with the photographic complement. The preparation of this book would certainly have not been possible without the understanding of our families, who always supported us in the pursuit of our fancy. Not least, we also wish to thank our publisher, Eugen Ulmer Verlag, for accommodating changes we wished to make for this new edition.

We hope this book will again be welcomed by lovebird fanciers and that it will provide useful advice to many.

Autumn, 1984

JÜRGEN BROCKMANN (Ahaus)
WERNER LANTERMANN (Oberhausen)

Lovebirds, Our
Favorite Small Parrots

Even in bygone times parrots and parakeets were among the most popular housepets of all. One of the first "imported" parrots must have been the Rose-ringed Parakeet (*Psittacula krameri*), which was brought to Europe by Alexander the Great around the middle of the fourth century B.C. Famed as well is Captain Cook's large Sulphur-crested Cockatoo (*Cacatua galerita*), which is said to have accompanied him in his travels around the world.

Nevertheless, only in the nineteenth century, and specifically at the beginning of the twentieth century, was parrot keeping undertaken methodically. Even though the first Budgerigars were traded already in 1840 at truly fantastic prices, these birds have in the meantime proved to be so fertile that today, despite a ban on their export by the Australian government, the number in captivity must greatly exceed those in the wild. At about the same time, many other parakeets and parrots from Africa, Asia, Australia, or South America were imported, so that after a short time a rich palette of diverse species and races could be chosen by the fancier for his aviaries.

Only relatively late, mostly at the beginning of the twentieth century, were lovebirds imported. For the most part, they proved to be easily bred and undemanding with respect to care. In addition, at times they were offered for sale in such numbers that nothing short of a boom in these small parrots took place.

In 1930, the much-debated parrot fever (psittacosis) and the resulting import prohibitions brought the entire parrot fancy to an end temporarily.

In the meantime, the restrictions have been relaxed. [In Germany], applications for a special license are granted by the appropriate veterinary authorities, who supervise the importation and trade of parrots. The applicant must be able to demonstrate expert knowledge and must provide segregated accommodations (quarantine stations) suitable for the prophylactic treatment of psittacosis in the imported parrots and to prevent the spread of the disease. Since the regulations differ in particulars in different states of the German Federal Republic, no detailed statements will be offered here. The interested parrot fancier should contact the appropriate authorities.

In addition, the prospective importer must act in conformity with the regulations of the lands of origin and the provisions of the species-protection laws when selecting the parrots to be imported. Many species of parrots and parakeets have become to a greater or lesser degree threatened with extinction in their homelands. The possibility of importation is regulated by the so-called Washington convention, or CITES treaty. All endangered wild animals are listed in one of the three appendixes of this treaty, according to the degree to which they are threatened. At the moment, lovebird species do not yet fall in the category with the most seriously endangered species, but are listed in Appendix Two of the treaty, as are all Psittaciformes (with the exception of the Budgerigar, the Cockatiel, and the Rose-ringed Parakeet).

With a body length of 13–17 cm, lovebirds, along with the parrotlets (*Forpus*) and the hanging-parrots (*Loriculus*), are among the smallest parrots in the world. Lovebirds are small, stockily built parrots that charm people with their agreeable temperaments and brilliant colors. Their voice is in some cases quite loud but in this respect they still fall considerably short of the larger parrots, so that they are well suited to apartments. The ground color of the plumage of all lovebirds is green. In some species both sexes have the same coloration, but one can accurately distinguish them in three species (*A. cana, A. taranta,* and *A. pullaria*).

Their popularity is based on various characteristics. Because of their small size, they require relatively little space. Since they are for the most part easy to breed, lovebirds are always affordable. In addition, they are quite attractively colored, and, finally, they are relatively undemanding with respect to diet and care. In any case, it should not be kept secret that some species, of the several that are kept, are relatively noisy, which should be considered, particularly with sensitive neighbors. Furthermore, they are sometimes quite quarrelsome among themselves and also with other birds.

Even so, the close social bonding, which both partners of a pair enter into for the duration of their lives, is appealing; they are not named *Unzertrennlichen* ('inseparables') for nothing. Furthermore, the genus name *Agapornis* is taken from the Greek and also means "lovebird." A pair of them do almost everything together. Characteristic too is the thorough head scratching, done in a fashion that can be observed in almost no other species of parrot. It is even claimed that their "love" toward each other goes so far that at the premature death of one of the partners the surviving bird will grieve and also die shortly thereafter. This, however, has never taken place in our establishment. Another conspecific, or if necessary even a Budgerigar, frequently helps to overcome the loss of a mate.

In summary it can be said that, provided one recognizes and accepts the lovebirds' minor vices, they are completely lovable and recommendable charges. Observing and comparing their distinctive living and nesting habits will continually charm the fancier as well as the breeder.

The following species and subspecies of the genus *Agapornis* are recognized: **Peach-faced Lovebird, *A. roseicollis*:** *A. r. roseicollis* (Vieillot); *A. r. catumbella* Hall. **Lovebirds with White Orbital Rings, *A. personata*:** Masked Lovebird, *A. p. personata* Reichenow; Fischer's Lovebird, *A. p. fischeri* Reichenow; Black-cheeked Lovebird, *A. p. nigrigenis* Sclater; Nyasa Lovebird, *A. p. lilianae* (Shelley). **Black-winged Lovebird, *A. taranta*:** *A. t. taranta* (Stanley); *A. t. nana* Neumann. **Grey-headed Lovebird, *A. cana*:** *A. c. cana* (Gmelin); *A. c. ablectanea* Bangs. **Black-collared Lovebird, *A. swinderniana*:** *A. s. swinderniana* (Kuhl); *A. s. zenkeri* Reichenow; *A. s. emini* Neumann. **Red-faced Lovebird, *A. pullaria*:** *A. p. pullaria* (Linné); *A. p. ugandae* Neumann.

As is apparent from this list, the genus *Agapornis* Selby consists of six species, and in each case various races are also recognized. For the sake of completeness, it should also be mentioned that some authors divide the genus into nine species, treating the forms with white orbital rings as four separate species. We personally prefer to view the *personata-fischeri-nigrigenis-lilianae* group as a single species with four subspecies. Admittedly, there is considerable variation in their coloration as well as in their size, but, even so, the lovebirds with white orbital rings are so similar in their body structure, behavior, and nesting habits that it is difficult to see them as separate species. In addition, their willingness to hybridize among themselves is a relatively certain sign of subspecific relationship. No doubt crosses between other species of lovebirds also succeed, but this is always accompanied by difficulties (Lantermann 1982).

Their Homeland and
Life in the Wild

With the exception of Grey-headed Lovebirds, which are found on Madagascar and several neighboring islands, all species of the genus live on the African mainland, for the most part near the equator. Except for Black-collared Lovebirds, which are exclusively forest dwellers, all lovebirds favor as living space dry savanna regions without true highland forests.

Peach-faced Lovebird, *A. roseicollis*. These birds have a relatively large range on the west coast of southern Africa, where one finds them in open, dry, mountainous scrubland up to an elevation of 1600 meters. They are extraordinarily abundant there; at the time when the maize is ripe, they invade cultivated areas by the hundreds. As a rule, however, one sees them in small flocks in the vicinity of a water hole. They feed on seeds, berries, and fruits.

In their homeland they breed in February and March. Peach-faced Lovebirds are looked upon as colony breeders. They nest in niches in cliffs or building recesses, and frequently also in the communal nests of weaver birds (a few of the nest chambers are used by the parrots, while the remainder remain in possession of the weavers). Ornithologists have observed how Peach-faced Lovebirds seized possession of the nest and then prevented the legitimate owners from entering.

The symbiosis of Peach-faced Lovebirds and weavers does not appear to be limited to a particular species of weaver, as Peach-faced Lovebirds have been found in the communal nests of various species of weavers. As nesting material the animals use small twigs and pieces of bark, which are carried to the nest by the female in her feathers. If they breed in weaver nests, however, then they leave the chamber unaltered and do not bring in new material.

Lovebirds with White Orbital Rings, *A. personata*. These have a relatively small range. Their homeland is arid savanna with isolated stands of trees but lacking true highland forests. According to Forshaw, the

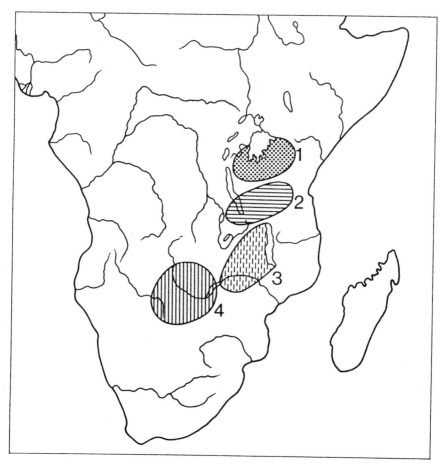

Range of *Agapornis personata:*
1, *A. p. fischeri;* 2, *A. p. personata;*
3, *A. p. lilianae;* 4, *A. p. nigrigenis.*

ranges of the four subspecies are supposed to be so exactly distinct from each other that the smallest distance between two subspecies is at least 65 kilometers. The ranges of *A. p. nigrigenis* and *A. p. lilianae* are separated by a distance of 160 kilometers. However, other authors speak of overlapping ranges, in which hybrids of the various subspecies may be observed.

The diet of these four subspecies consists principally of various grass and weed seeds and of maize in the milk-ripe stage. In addition, berries, fruits, grains, and buds are readily taken as dietary supplements.

Masked Lovebird, *A. p. personata*. This form lives in northeastern Tanzania, from Lake Manyara to the highlands of Iringa. In addition, they were introduced in Dar es Salaam and in Nairobi (Kenya). They are found in sparsely wooded savanna (at altitudes between 1100 and 1700 meters), broken up by scattered tall acacias. During the period from March to August they build their nests in hollow trees, niches in buildings, etc. Now and then they also breed in abandoned swallow nests. They too are colony breeders. The nests are built almost exclusively by the females, using long twigs, strips of bark, and blades of grass, among other items, as nesting materials. As with all other lovebirds with white orbital rings, the building materials are carried to the nest in the bill.

Fischer's Lovebird, *A. p. fischeri*. Inhabitants of a biotope very similar to that occupied by the Masked Lovebird, their range is located south of Lake Victoria in northern Tanzania. They also occur at altitudes between 1000 and 1700 meters. Living in small flocks, they are found in the previously mentioned savanna as well as in cultivated farmland, where large flocks congregate when the grain is ripe. They are colony breeders that start to prepare their nests for breeding at the beginning of May. They also nest in hollow trees, on buildings, and under the leaves of large palm trees. In addition, the animals are also found in the communal nests of weaver birds. Nest construction is like that of the Masked Lovebird.

Nyasa Lovebird, *A. p. lilianae*. Found in southern Tanzania, northeastern Mozambique, and Zambia; from time to time they can also be found in Malawi and in Zimbabwe/Rhodesia. They prefer altitudes between 600 and 1000 meters; possibly they wander to higher elevations outside the breeding season. As a rule, they are found in scrubland with sparse acacia growth, but occasionally they encroach upon cultivated farmland. In addition to grass seeds, berries, and buds, the animals also feed on ripe grain, millets, and acacia seeds. They spend a large part of the day on the ground in search of food. A water hole is also visited several times a day. In January and February, Nyasa Lovebirds breed in hollow trees and frequently also in the vicinity of human settlements. In Luangwa in Zambia, birds were found breeding in weaver nests.

Black-cheeked Lovebird, *A. p. nigrigenis*. Their range extends from southwestern Zambia in the east to Livingstone in the north. Occasion-

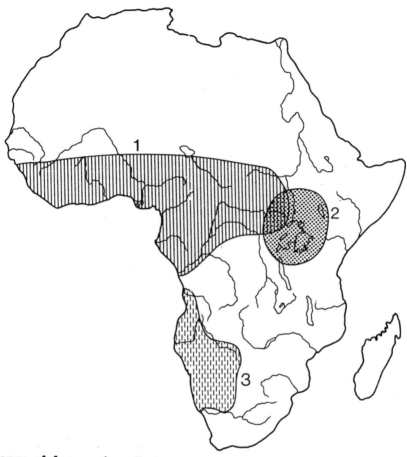

**Range of *Agapornis pullaria*
and *A. roseicollis*:**
1, *A. p. pullaria;*
2, *A. p. ugandae;*
3, *A. r. roseicollis*
and *A. r. catumbella.*

ally, the animals are also encountered in the extreme western part of
Zimbabwe/Rhodesia as far as Victoria Falls. Black-cheeked Lovebirds
live in lowlands, inhabiting a biotope similar to that of the Nyasa Lovebird. In their breeding habits and diet the animals entirely resemble the
other races of the species *Agapornis personata.* As a result of trapping
and selling, the population has been severely reduced in their
homeland.

**Range of *Agapornis taranta*
and *A. swinderniana*:**
1, *A. t. taranta;*
2, *A. t. nana;*
3, *A. s. swinderniana;*
4, *A. s. zenkeri.*

Black-winged Lovebird, *A. taranta.* These lovebirds occur in small groups in the highlands of Abyssinia at altitudes between 1300 and 3200 meters, where the flocks (three to twenty birds) inhabit the crowns of junipers. These birds are seldom found in the vicinity of human settlements; they lack the ability to associate closely with people, as is done by several other species. Like *A. pullaria* and *A. cana*, this species can be viewed as an avoider of cultivation. Dilger, in his article

"The comparative ethology of the African parrot genus *Agapornis*," supplies some interesting facts on this theme. Moreau considers the *taranta-cana-pullaria* group to be the most primitive in the genus *Agapornis*.

Their living spaces differ somewhat from those of the other lovebirds. In their Ethiopian homeland they live in open woodlands, which are overgrown with *Hagenia*, *Juniperus*, and *Hypericum*. They have also been observed in acacias and euphorbias. They spend the night in tree hollows, possibly in woodpecker holes, which are utilized throughout the entire year. Every morning they fly in flocks to search for food, only to return again to their sleeping holes shortly before darkness. Black-winged Lovebirds feed on seeds, fruits, and berries. Juniper berries and the seeds of a particular species of fig (*Ficus sycamorus*) are enjoyed especially.

In October the females build their nest chambers. In decayed tree cavities or in the roosting trees just mentioned, a small nesting substrate is built of twigs, blades of grass, etc. The materials are carried to the nest by the female.

Grey-headed Lovebird, A. cana. These are the only lovebirds that do not live on the African mainland. Both races live in coastal regions of the island of Madagascar, as well as the islands Mauritius, Rodriguez, Zanzibar, and the Seychelles. They favor open savanna, frequently in the vicinity of evergreen woodland.

As a rule, they are seen in small flocks of five to twenty animals, often in the company of species of small finches. In some regions they are unusually abundant, but still are considered to be shy. According to Forshaw, unlike *A. personata* and *A. roseicollis*, they are not close followers of cultivation. Their principal food is grass seeds. They also take small amounts of grain, rice, and various fruits. They spend most of each day searching for food.

Grey-headed Lovebirds nest during the rainy season, between November and April. The hens build small nesting substrate from blades of grass, leaves, and pieces of bark in tree cavities. As a rule, the clutch consists of four eggs.

Black-collared Lovebird, A. swinderniana. These distinctly woodland birds roam in small parties (up to twelve animals) through the forests in search of food. Their diet consists principally of figs and rice (Forshaw).

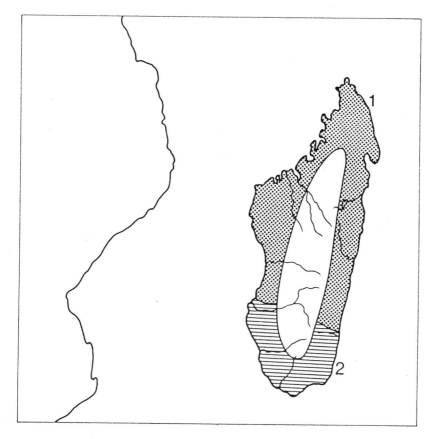

Range of _Agapornis cana_ on Madagascar:
1, _A. c. cana;_ 2, _A. c. ablectanea._

The genus _Agapornis_ was erected in 1826 by O. J. Selby from the only specimen (a prepared skin) available at that time, which was a Black-collared Lovebird. Yet these birds have hardly ever been imported, even to the present day. According to Stresemann, this is due to the fact that this species rarely comes to the ground in search of food and is therefore difficult to capture. Another difficulty seems to be caused by the diet of these animals. In the Congo, Père Hutsebout could keep this species alive only if a particular kind of wild fig was available; otherwise they died within three or four days. According to

17

Cunningham-van Someren, other possible foods are said to be *Ficus* fruits and half-ripe, milky maize (Forshaw).

Forshaw gives their range as western and central Africa. The breeding season of *A. swinderniana* falls in July. The nest chambers are, as with *A. pullaria*, built in the nests of arboreal termites.

Red-faced Lovebird, *A. pullaria*. Having the most extensive range of any of the lovebirds, this species is found throughout all of central Africa, although they undoubtedly prefer open-savanna landscapes, while in most cases highland forests are avoided. On the islands of Principe and Fernando Po this species is considered to be extinct (Forshaw).

They live in small flocks in thickly overgrown and semi-open savanna landscapes. Like most of the members of the genus *Agapornis*, they principally feed on the seeds of grasses and weeds, which they readily take from the ground. Forshaw cites dietary supplements such as berries, fruits, and wild figs.

In Uganda and Tanzania the breeding season begins in May. In other regions, however, sitting females have been observed between October and February. In contrast to other lovebirds, the animals nest in termite colonies, usually those found in trees, less commonly in the mounds on the ground. The nest chamber is located at the end of a long tunnel, which the animals dig themselves with the aid of bills and feet. Dilger reports that the females primarily undertake the excavation of the nest chamber; though the cocks frequently try to help, they are usually unsuccessful. As with *A. cana* and *A. taranta*, the nest chamber is furnished with a small substrate of blades of grass, twigs, etc.

Accommodations,
Diet, and Illness

Some Initial Guidelines

In complete contrast to some other species of parrots, well-acclimated lovebirds are relatively problemfree to keep and some can even be bred. Nevertheless, it would be advisable for one to first gain some experience with the even less problematical Budgerigar before purchasing any lovebirds. It is also advisable to "step up" to keeping and breeding lovebirds by starting with Peach-faced Lovebirds (*A. r. roseicollis*), Masked Lovebirds (*A. p. personata*), or Fischer's Lovebirds (*A. p. fischeri*), because with these forms in particular one has a reasonable expectation of breeding success before long. In addition, these three forms can always be obtained at reasonable prices from domestic breeders. In any case, for the beginner only domestically bred animals, and not newly imported ones, are recommended, since imported ones must first carefully be settled in with an appropriate diet and acclimation, as losses caused by unsuitable housing and care would be painful.

At this point we wish to mention the responsibility that the animal keeper assumes. From the moment of purchase, he takes on an unavoidable duty to the captive creature, which has been subjugated totally against its will. For this reason, before one decides to purchase an animal, one must conscientiously weigh the advantages and disadvantages, with the realization that keeping any animal will demand a definite amount of one's spare time in the future. One should also consult one or another of the specialized books on the topic beforehand (see the Bibliography), so that at least the worst errors can be avoided. Whoever is not prepared to do this will sooner or later also find it burdensome to have to care for his charges—the animals are always the ones that suffer. Anyone who only wants from time to time to see a "pretty parrot" should instead go to the zoo on Sundays.

Accommodations

In general, there are four possible ways of keeping lovebirds: housing them in cages, in indoor flights, in flights outdoors, and keeping them at liberty.

Keeping them in **cages** is certainly the most widely practiced method. The reasons for this are quite obvious, for who really has enough room to be able to build expensive outdoor flights? Preferably, the cages should be enclosed on three sides and should have a rectangular floor. The so-called box cage can be purchased in shops almost everywhere. Nevertheless, it is better and cheaper to build a suitable cage yourself. An appropriate size would be 80 × 50 × 50 centimeters for a pair that possibly may breed. However, a flight cage for several young animals should have a size of approximately one cubic meter. Particle board with a thickness of 16 millimeters (perhaps with plastic veneer) is splendidly suited for this purpose, since it is cheap and easy to work. The majority of lovebird keepers avoid using wood as the construction material for cages on the grounds that it will sooner or later fall victim to the bills of the occupants. However, this is patently incorrect. Naturally, all accessible edges will be quickly "rounded off" by the animals, but even lovebirds will not tackle a smooth surface.

If one builds one's cages with some skill, they will serve their purpose for many years. A nonpoisonous, durable, and nonreflective lacquer (the best is white matt lacquer) is suitable for the interior of the cage. In any case, the particle board must be painted twice because the first coat will be partially absorbed. Cages veneered with plastic are ideal, of course, but they are decidedly more expensive. Cages of particle board that have been painted twice are just as easy to keep clean as the veneered ones.

For covering the front of the cage, spot-welded galvanized wire mesh (12 × 12 or 12 × 25 mm), which does not rust and is quite sturdy, is recommended. In addition, the cage fronts which are available commercially are also suitable. Thinned bitumen lacquer, which remains elastic and does not peel off after drying as is the case with normal lacquer, should be used for painting the wire. Bitumen lacquer can always be obtained inexpensively from roofers. Of course, such painting is not absolutely necessary, but it does provide a better view of the birds (with reflective galvanized wire this is not the case, even though it will darken in the course of time).

It is best to furnish the cage with three food dishes, a water receptacle, and a bathing dish. In case you don't yet know, all lovebirds bathe with genuine passion!

It is useful to equip any cage with a food tray (which is accessible from the outside) in which the food dishes can be placed securely. In this way, one does not have to disturb the animals more than absolutely necessary for the daily feeding. It is also advisable to equip the cage with a tray approximately 7 cm high to catch the droppings, so that it can be more easily cleaned.

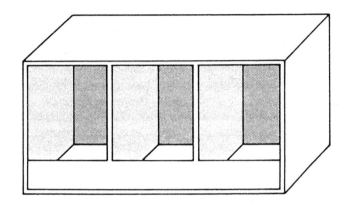

Roosting boxes for lovebirds.

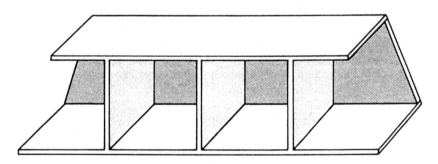

Roosting boxes are suitable for communal cages and flights. With these one will quickly be able to pick out compatible pairs (even with young animals). If two birds sit together in a compartment at twilight and during the night, one can infer with some certainty that they are a pair.

A bright corner of a room would be a suitable location for a single cage, but one should always keep in mind that the birds (if housed in an unsuitable cage) can make a considerable mess in the room. Never choose the kitchen, especially not a kitchen cabinet, as the permanent location for your darlings, for no living creature can endure all of the kitchen odors for any length of time. The cage should stand at eye level if possible (so that the birds feel more secure), and should be placed so that it is not in the sunlight the entire day. The occupants must of course also have the opportunity to retire to the shade.

For interested parties with greater ambitions, those wishing to keep a number of animals and to build up a breeding stock, a bright room or attic is recommended, where several cages can be placed atop and beside one another. Such a breeding installation can be constructed by oneself in any size and form without difficulty.

Indoor flights are another, truly ideal arrangement for keeping lovebirds. They are available in all sizes and price ranges, or are easily constructed from ordinary lumber and the wire mesh mentioned previously. The size, of course, depends on the space available and the number of birds. Flights large enough so that one can comfortably go inside through a door are preferable, because, based on experience, cleanliness and tidiness suffer when one can only enter and service the enclosure in a bent posture. A size of 1 m wide, 2 m deep, and 2 m high is completely sufficient. If several flights of this kind stand in a row, then the sides adjacent to one another must both be covered with wire mesh (the space between the mesh must be at least 5 cm) to prevent biting. In a flight of the shape and size just described, three breeding pairs of one kind of lovebird can easily be kept and bred if the animals are all introduced into the flight at the same time. One requirement, of course, is a sufficient number of nest sites. For two pairs, at least three nest boxes should be provided. It is also advisable to hang up boxes for young birds that have left the nest, which they may like to sleep in and which can also serve as places of refuge. The boxes must also be placed as far apart as possible to prevent neighborly quarrels among the animals.

With accommodations of this kind, one has the opportunity of installing a larger feeding station with a landing perch. In this regard, refer to af Enejhelm (1968), who suggests constructing a kind of feeding shelf from doubled, sturdy rectangular wire mesh, on which the various dishes can be placed. A feeding station of this kind always stays clean (the empty seed hulls fall through the wire mesh to the floor of the flight) and can be serviced from the outside if it is designed appropriately.

It goes without saying that an indoor aviary should receive sufficient light during the greater part of the day and should also have some direct sunlight as well. Even so, the room must also be equipped with lights, so that the day can be lengthened on dreary autumn and winter afternoons (energy-saving fluorescent tubes are very suitable for this).

Keeping birds in **outdoor flights**, provided it is done correctly, is the best way to house our parrots, since conditions in outdoor flights no doubt are the nearest approach to a natural way of life. In any event, one must take note of various points, to derive genuine pleasure from an aviary.

As a rule, an aviary consists of a shelter room to which a flight is connected. In our case the flight area should have dimensions of approximately 1.5 × 3 m, while for the shelter room approximately 1.5 × 2 m is completely sufficient. If space is limited, a smaller flight than stated is also adequate. A variety of materials can be used for building: for example, asbestos-concrete sheets, wood, glass, and stone. No doubt the choice will be primarily determined by the financial resources of the fancier. Appropriately, one should begin building the aviary with a solid concrete base, which should extend at least 80 cm into the ground. The shelter room is best built from durable bricks, and should be insulated as well as possible (styrofoam or fiberglass, or both). A good roof can be easily constructed from asbestos-concrete panels or transparent corrugated sheets, or one can use the much cheaper, traditional roofing felt. The shelter room, if possible, should have a passage, approximately 1 m wide, from which the aviary can be serviced. Furthermore, it is almost mandatory to equip this area with electricity, water, and, above all, a source of heat. Heating an aviary of this sort can be accomplished in various ways. The simplest and at the same time most economical (if it is well insulated) is a connection to the central heating of the house. In other cases, electric or oil heaters provide good service. It is best to place these appliances in the passage mentioned previously, so that there is no danger of the animals getting burned. In other respects the shelter room is furnished much like an indoor flight.

The flight itself is attached directly to the shelter room and should rest on a solid foundation to prevent any troublesome gnawers from gaining entry. With the aid of dowels and screws, a sturdy wooden frame can easily be fastened to the foundation. The framework should of course be painted with a wood-impregnating agent. Here too it is appropriate to use galvanized rectangular wire mesh, which must be fastened on the inside of the framework to protect the wooden parts from the animals' bills. This time it is necessary to coat the wire mesh to prevent too much oxidation, because, left untreated, even galvanized wire mesh will not last forever. With the help of a paint roller, even large areas of wire mesh can effortlessly be provided with a durable coating. For protection against bad weather, at least a third of the flight area should be provided with a roof, preferably of window glass or plexiglass sheets. If need be, any other weather-resistant, transparent material may be used.

Poured concrete is best for the floor of the shelter room. In the flight, tiles can be laid or the ground can simply be covered with a thick layer of sand. In both cases, an adequate substrate is an absolute necessity. In any case, at least once a year the earth must be dug out to a depth of at least 30 cm and replaced.

Furnishing such an aviary presents no problems. Small, many-branched trees or limbs (fruit tree, willow), of a strength that will accommodate the sizes of the parrots to be cared for, will do for perching. At the same time they allow the birds to gnaw (keeping them occupied) and also stimulate digestion. Additionally, they can be easily replaced at any time. The feeding station and the nest boxes should be located in the shelter room if possible. Communication between the shelter room and the flight outside is provided by an opening approximately 20 × 20 cm, which must be closable. It goes without saying that the food dishes as well as the bathing dish should not be placed under the perches, so that they do not become too badly soiled.

The various questions about details that pose themselves when building an aviary on one's own can be solved by a fairly skilled craftsman after some reflection. It would exceed the scope of this book to provide complete construction plans for various kinds of aviaries. For particulars, refer to specialized books such as Aschenborn's.

The last, and by far the most difficult sort of lovebird keeping is keeping them at **liberty**. Innumerable attempts have sought to make it possible to keep these small parrots completely without bars. Of course, an undertaking of this kind can only be carried out in very rural regions where the manifold dangers of civilization (as, for example, traffic, etc.) are for the most part absent. It is best to begin an experiment of this kind in the following manner: One places a pair that have proved themselves able to rear young (never a young pair) in a sheltered cage in the garden to breed. The cage must be set up in such a way that no intruders (for example, cats, rats, and mice) can disturb the animals, but the birds should still be able to survey the area. The experiment should be conducted only at a time when abundant food is available in the wild for the animals. Nevertheless, be careful of fruit trees and grain fields that have been sprayed with insecticides.

As soon as there are young in the nest that have been fed well for several days, the wire mesh can be removed from the front of the cage. As a rule, the parents will at first attempt short excursions, and later quite prolonged ones, from which they will in most cases return (because of the strong feeding drive) to care for their young. Nevertheless, one should continue to provide the bird family with sufficient food. As soon as the youngsters become self-sufficient, there is relatively great danger that the birds will temporarily or even permanently wander to other areas. Therefore, one should recapture the parents, generally shortly before the young leave the nest. This is best done at night, when both parents sleep in the nest box anyway.

By no means do we wish to recommend this method of keeping, since it can certainly lead to quite high losses, whether the parents fly away or are poisoned by sprayed fruit. Because of their conspicuous coloration, the parrots can also easily fall prey to predators. This is merely an interesting experiment, for which the responsibility must lie with each individual.

At present [in Germany] there is no law that expressly prohibits keeping of parrots at liberty. The amendment to the federal environmental conservation act, which appeared on January 1, 1981, nevertheless states the following in this connection (§44): "Animals foreign to an area may neither be released nor settled into the wild." Our case is certainly not a release of animals. Settlement of the birds in our opinion is also out of the question, because the keeper does not intend to leave the lovebirds in the surrounding biotope the entire year and in so doing attempt to naturalize them. On the contrary, he will as before be concerned with the well-being of his charges, because he knows they would not be in a position to adapt to the actual living conditions.

If one wishes to undertake an experiment of this kind, it is better to take a less valuable breeding pair and reckon with their loss from the start. To be sure, to successfully keep lovebirds at liberty would be a special experience for any bird fancier, although there would certainly be trouble with the neighbors on account of the gnawed fruit trees.

Diet and Nutrition

The cardinal rule in the keeping of animals (in this case, parrots) in captivity should and must be to offer a diet that is as varied as possible. Of course, one is never in a position to obtain the kind of variety of foods the animals could find if they were free. Nonetheless, there is a whole series of possibilities for developing a varied menu for the birds.

The principal food of lovebirds is small seeds. Thus it is possible to prepare a mixture of a good-quality Budgerigar mixture, oats, wild-bird seed, silver millet, and canary seed that is readily accepted by most lovebirds. In addition, sunflower seeds should be offered occasionally in a separate dish. A serviceable large-parakeet mixture can be obtained in almost all pet shops.

Another essential food, which can be particularly valuable in winter (which is the "vitamin-deficient season") and during the breeding season, is sprouted seeds. Oats, wheat, sunflower, millet, etc. are suitable. The preparation of sprouted food is relatively simple when done as follows:

One places the amount needed in a container with water, so that the seeds are covered with water, and then leaves them for twenty-four hours. Next, one puts the seeds in a sieve, rinses them thoroughly, and spreads them on small wire-covered frames (stacked atop one another approximately 2–3 cm apart). It is best to equip these frames with small feet, so that air can circulate from all sides. After one or two days more, one again rinses the seeds thoroughly and then feeds them to the animals. The seeds have by now germinated and possess a relatively high vitamin content. One should nevertheless guard against the appearance of mold, which could produce intestinal illness in the birds. The use of a 1% formalin solution while rinsing the seeds prevents the growth of this mold. In the winter, first-rate green food can be easily prepared by sowing oats, wheat, millet, or sunflower seeds in small trays and then feeding the germinated seedlings (approximately 3–4 cm high) to the birds. In addition, the birds should also receive fruit, berries, and greens daily. Of the fruits, apples are readily available at all times of year. More desirable, however, are pears and carrots. Of the berries, rosehips and rowan berries, which can also be frozen, can be obtained in the summer and the autumn. One can list a genuinely varied selection under the heading of greens (see the accompanying table). Common parsley, which has the highest vitamin content of all, is not eaten by all birds. Also suitable are chicory, dandelion, spinach, mangel, and chickweed. When feeding ordinary lettuce, one should certainly keep in mind that it consists mostly of water and therefore is not very nutritious. (Beware of sprayed vegetables!).

A very valuable food, which is readily taken by most parrots, is half-ripe (milky) maize. Unfortunately, maize is only available in late summer. Whoever owns a freezer, however, can freeze sufficient amounts for the winter. It is advisable to begin by feeding very small quantities, since suddenly supplementing the diet with food of this kind can easily lead to difficulties in digestion.

When they are accustomed to it, all lovebirds very readily eat the egg food that is available on the market, particularly when rearing young. One can easily mix the egg food with sprouted seed, but one must be careful that the food does not become sour or moldy.

In addition, feeding a mineral supplement is essential. Mineral blocks or cuttlebones provide the essential minerals and trace elements required by the animals. To cover the floor of the cage, one should also use a good bird sand with seashells added.

It is certainly self-evident that the birds should receive fresh water at least once a day. Through soiled water dishes, disease germs (only one bird need be ill) can quickly spread to the entire population. A few drops of a calcium preparation (such as Avisanol) can be added to the drinking water daily; it both sterilizes and mineralizes the water.

Finally, let it be said that the animals should be given fresh fruit-tree or willow twigs for gnawing at least once a week. This prevents boredom and serves to whet the bill. In addition, valuable substances that serve to keep the birds healthy (regulating the bowels) are found in the bark.

If one provides a quite varied diet (greens, sprouted seeds, and egg food), as a rule additional vitamin preparations are not necessary. But

Nutritional Composition of Certain Vegetables									
Nutrients in a 100-gram portion	Head Lettuce	Chicory	Spinach	Mangel	Lamb's Quarters	Parsley	Carrot	Red Beet	Radish
Principal Components									
Protein (g)	1.2	1.7	2.4	2.1	1.8	4.4	1.0	1.5	1.0
Fat (g)	0.2	0.2	0.4	0.3	0.4	0.4	0.2	0.1	0.1
Carbohydrate (g)	1.7	2.0	2.4	2.9	2.6	9.8	7.3	7.6	3.5
Minerals									
Iron (mg)	0.6	1.4	3.0	2.7	2.0	8.0	0.7	0.9	1.5
Sodium (mg)	8	50	60	90	4	30	45	86	17
Potassium (mg)	220	350	660	380	420	1000	280	340	255
Calcium (mg)	20	50	110	100	30	240	35	30	34
Phosphorus (mg)	35	50	48	40	50	130	30	45	26
Vitamins									
A (I.U.)	1,500	900	8,200	5,900	7,000	12,080	13,500	180	38
B_1 (mcg)	60	52	86	100	65	140	70	22	33
B_2 (mcg)	90	120	240	160	80	300	55	40	30
C (mg)	10	9	47	40	30	170	6	10	30

with house pets that are fed exclusively with seeds, vitamin-deficiency illnesses do occur very frequently, since particularly the vitamins A, B₁, D, E, and carotene quickly lose their potency with prolonged storage.

Numerous good vitamin preparations, which one can spread on the food or add to drinking water, are available commercially. When purchasing these, one should pay attention to the expiration date. Overdosing is hardly possible; only large amounts of vitamin A or D over a long period of time will produce symptoms of illness.

Some kinds of egg food are enriched with unsaturated fatty acids and essential amino acids, which the body itself cannot produce. The supplemental feeding of amino acids of this kind appears to us to be particularly important.

Illnesses

Although well-acclimated lovebirds, like all parrots, are relatively robust birds, from time to time it can still happen that some become ill. One should make it a rule to closely examine one's stock once a day, and to look at each bird, in order to be able to isolate any animal that appears to be ill as quickly as possible, so that the entire stock is not endangered. A group of birds can be tended and cared for well only when the size of the population corresponds to the keeper's available free time. For the conscientious bird fancier with normally restricted free time, ten to fifteen pairs would certainly be enough. In this case, at least an hour and a half is required daily. If the number of birds gets out of hand, experience shows, the necessary cleaning of the cages and flights will be neglected, and an ideal growth medium for bacteria will quickly build up on the cage floors. A thick layer of droppings on the floor of the cage literally courts disaster. For this reason, the first commandment is to maintain the greatest cleanliness possible. Even so, it can happen from time to time that a bird nevertheless becomes ill. Unfortunately, in birds the symptoms are seldom characteristic enough to allow the diagnosis of a particular disease. In most cases, the animals merely sit with fluffed feathers on the floor in a corner of the cage or the flight, or in front of the food dish, and sleep. Their eyes lack the usual brightness. Sick animals also frequently sleep on both legs (healthy ones shift their body weight to one leg while sleeping).

The first step is to isolate the bird immediately. It is advisable to have a so-called hospital cage available when illness occurs. These cages are always available from breeders' suppliers, although the prices are not inconsiderable. Resourceful home craftsmen can build just as suitable a cage themselves. The hospital cage is almost exactly like the ordinary box cage. The front is enclosed with a pane of glass, but, when the bird's health has improved, it can be replaced with wire mesh. Ventilation slits are found on the side walls. They should be off-set, so that no drafts can develop. A small, wire-covered frame can serve as the floor of the cage, so that the bird's droppings can fall to a linen cloth underneath. It is best if the food dishes are inserted from the outside.

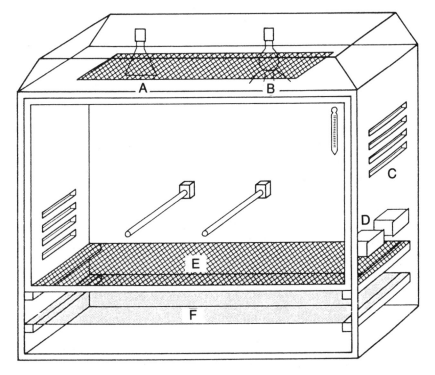

Hospital cage: *A,* heating element; *B,* light bulb; *C,* ventilation slots; *D,* food cups; *E,* mesh floor; *F,* removable cloth to catch droppings.

In the roof of the cage a large slit is sawed, and then covered with wire mesh. Over this a hood, such as those used for aquariums and ter-rariums, can be placed, and heat lamps and fluorescent tubes installed inside. It is recommended that lamps of various strengths be used, so that suitable combinations of several bulbs will produce various temperature levels. Of course, each of the heat lamps must have its own switch. Before being used for the first time, the temperature levels must be checked as accurately as possible with a thermometer placed inside the cage.

In most cases, it is sufficient to keep the ill bird in such a cage for a short time at medium-strength heat (approximately 28 C.). Its diet should consist of a dry-seed mixture only. In the beginning, water should be withheld completely. Instead, one should offer lukewarm, unsweetened chamomile tea. If the bird's condition has not improved after about two days, then one should seek the advice of an experienced veterinarian. There are several kinds of antibiotics which can have a beneficial effect in these cases. With the lovebirds' slight body weight, however, the dosage is so small that it is better for the layman not to conduct his own experiments.

The illnesses of lovebirds can have many causes: e.g., drafts; extreme temperature changes in the bird's living quarters; or unsuitable, nutritionally deficient, or spoiled food. Psychological disturbances (for example, change of location, capture, dominance fighting) can also lead to a weakening of resistance, making the animals particularly susceptible to illness.

External Injuries

Fractures of the Bones and Wings. Fractures of the extremities occur relatively seldom with our small parrots. If a limb has been fractured, it should be returned to its original position and immobilized as much as possible, since otherwise the break will not heal. Splints, whether of wood or something else, only make sense with the leg bones or the toes. In all other kinds of fractures complete immobilization will not be achieved in this way. In such cases, the leg or wing is fixed to the body with a bandage of adhesive tape. As a rule, the period of healing is short. But difficulties frequently come up because, experience shows, parrots "work on" bandages, leg splints, etc., until they have freed themselves.

Minor Injuries Minor injuries normally give no reason for concern. Light bleeding can be staunched with ferric chloride or Arterenol (norepinephrine-HCl, Hoechst). Usually, no other treatment is necessary. As a rule, there is no danger of infection.

Animals with more severe wounds (head injuries, for example) are best referred to the veterinary specialist, who will then either stitch them or treat them some other way.

Parasitic Diseases

Ectoparasites. Externally appearing parasites are the red mite (*Dermanyssus avium*), mange mites (which belong to the group of burrowing mites), and feather lice (Mallophaga). If blood-sucking parasites, such as mites, for example, appear in large numbers, they present an immediate danger to our charges and under certain circumstances can lead to death.

Preventive measures consist of the greatest possible cleanliness and regular disinfection of the living quarters. For this purpose, commercial preparations (such as AF 404 or Vigorid) have proved excellent. Treatment entails the repeated use of an insecticide. For the treatment of skin mites, Odylen (mesulphen, Bayer) is the choice.

Innumerable remedies are available commercially, so no universally applicable directions for use can be given here. It is absolutely necessary to make sure, however, that the preparations used state on the package that they are expressly formulated for use with birds. Sprays should be used only for perches and the like. Spraying the plumage should always be avoided. For application to the plumage, powders—for example, Alugan (brommethylhexachlorbicyclohepten, Hoechst) and Bolfo (carbamate, Bayer), among others—are better. In many cases it is advisable not to allow the animals or their food supplies to come in contact with these agents.

Endoparasites. Other parasites which have appeared more frequently in recent times are worms. We distinguish roundworms (ascarids), threadworms (*Capillaria*), and cecal worms (*Heterakis*).

A worm infestation is not always detectable. Thus if the equilibrium between host and parasite is broken, the bird can lie dead in the cage one morning without a visible cause. A slight disturbance of the bird's nutritional state may mean that the parasites can no longer be held in check. Psychological causes can also be responsible for the endoparasites gaining the upper hand. Worm eggs in the animal's feces can be seen under the microscope without difficulty. For this reason, one should have feces of one's entire stock analyzed once a year.

Various preparations are effective remedies; as a rule, they are given to the animals in the drinking water. For roundworms and threadworms, levamisole (Concurat, Bayer) and fenbendazole (Panacur, Hoechst) are suitable. The less frequently encountered tapeworms are controlled with niclosamide (Yomesan, Bayer). Certain preparations (such as antibiotics) are quite difficult to administer because of the lovebirds' small body weight, and are not tolerated particularly well. For this reason, it is suggested that one always consult an experienced veterinarian.

Infectious Diseases

In addition to various bacterial infections and those caused by fungus (aspergillosis), viral diseases are also found in psittacines. To protect your own stock against the introduction of an infection, newly purchased animals should without fail be held in quarantine and observed closely for a minimum of fourteen days. The floor of the cage is temporarily covered with glossy white paper, to make apparent any changes in the droppings.

One of the most familiar and at the same time most dangerous infectious illnesses is parrot fever (psittacosis), which has been known since 1930. It was first introduced into Germany by amazon parrots from South America. As a result, the federal government at that time instituted a strict import embargo for all species of parrots, which has recently been relaxed again, fortunately. In general, one can assume that all of the imported birds on the market have put a forty-five-day quarantine period behind them and are therefore free of pathogens. As previously, birds from Dutch wholesale firms present a danger, for the quarantine period in the Netherlands is shorter than the incubation period of psittacosis. The pathogen causing parrot fever has also been found in many other kinds of birds (for instance, pigeons, ducks, gulls, petrels, etc.); in such cases one speaks of "ornithosis."

Unfortunately, the disease has no characteristic symptoms. Watery droppings, fluffed plumage, dull eyes, irregular breathing, and conspicuous, sudden tameness can be signs of this illness. It can take two different courses: On the one hand, it can lead to deaths without any symptoms of illness being observed in the animals. On the other, infected birds can shed the virus for months without appearing to be ill. These "latent" carriers are a great threat to the stock.

Thanks to its size, the psittacosis pathogen was discovered and isolated quite early. It was established that it can be fought with antibiotics. Since 1970, the treatment of infected stocks has been permitted. An outbreak of the disease should immediately be reported to the ap-

Peach-faced Lovebirds housed in an outdoor flight.

propriate veterinary inspection office. Treatment can only be undertaken with official supervision. Tetracycline is used. During treatment the animals must be given sufficient vitamins regularly. After its completion (approximately thirty days for *Agapornis* species), the droppings must be free of pathogens.

Infected parrots also present an acute danger of contagion to people. The incubation period lasts approximately seven to fourteen days. The disease manifests itself as a febrile lung infection, which should by no means be made light of. Again, tetracycline is used for treatment.

Other Pathological Conditions

Vitamin Deficiencies. Illnesses caused by vitamin deficiencies very seldom appear if the stock is well cared for. A suitable diet can prevent such illness. Administration of a multivitamin preparation, in serious cases by direct injection into the breast muscle, often leads to the animals' complete recovery.

Egg Binding. In egg binding, females are unable to lay a developed egg. Possible causes can be poor condition; overexertion through too much breeding; egg laying in chilly surroundings; calcium deficiency; and breeding when still young. Prevention is better than cure in every case. If one eliminates the causes just mentioned and provides a varied diet (with vitamins and minerals) and perhaps also some cod-liver oil, then egg binding will seldom occur. An ill bird sits with fluffed plumage on the floor of the cage and has swollen hindparts. By carefully exploring the belly region with the fingers, the normal egg in its calcium shell can be felt. In the animal's attempt to expel the egg, it occasionally happens that the oviduct prolapses along with the egg. Often this is caused by a rough shell. Prompt intervention is necessary or else the bird will die. One places it in a warmed hospital cage and then rubs its hindparts with a few drops of warmed oil, or trickles a few drops into the cloaca. As a rule, the egg is passed in a few hours, and the bird recovers quickly. Infrared irradiation is helpful, and there is no reason not to continue it for a while afterward. The lamp should be placed approximately 60 cm from the cage.

Feather Plucking. From time to time one sees lovebirds that pluck their own feathers, those of their mate, or those of still-dependent youngsters.

Possible causes are (a) inadequate diet; (b) boredom; (c) unfavorable climatic conditions (for example, extremely low humidity); (d) psychological disturbances; and (e) skin diseases.

With skin diseases, the skin of the areas of the body that are being plucked is often thickened and covered with yellowish deposits, scabs, and usually peck wounds as well. Skin inflammations are frequently quite difficult to treat, since pathogens such as fungi and bacteria have become resistant to many medicines. In stubborn cases, it is advisable to have a veterinarian make a skin smear to determine which salve or tincture will be effective. In the other four instances mentioned, the most important measure is to eliminate the cause; that is, the animals should be kept under substantially improved conditions. A balanced diet (animal protein, mealworms, hard-boiled egg, etc.) is important. Additionally, the birds should be provided with something to occupy themselves (fresh twigs for gnawing, mineral blocks). Most lovebirds also appreciate a daily shower.

Once the animals have begun to pluck feathers, it is difficult to cure them of the habit. Once again, prevention is better than having to find a remedy.

The Natural Molt

The molt that recurs yearly does not really belong with illnesses. Even so, there are certain things that keepers and breeders should pay attention to during the molt. The molt serves to renew the plumage at fixed intervals. During this time, however, the birds generally are neither unable to fly nor do they have noticeable gaps in their plumage. Therefore, when purchasing new birds, it is recommended that one examine the condition of their plumage very carefully. With imports, one often sees broken-off feathers and feather stumps. As a rule, these grow back again perfectly at the next molt. Even so, bare spots in the plumage should be examined more closely. Frequently, other causes are involved, not the molt, as is frequently claimed. During the molt, the birds' powers of resistance are greatly reduced. One should make allowances for this by providing an especially good diet and regular vitamin-and-mineral supplements. As a rule, the molt proceeds smoothly and is over with in a short time. With increasing age the color intensity of the plumage can also increase.

Red edging on a Peach-faced Lovebird's feathers most likely results from a dietary deficiency.

Facing page: Feather plucking by parents is a serious problem in lovebird breeding, evident here on the back of a Blue Masked Lovebird.

A young Lutino Peach-faced Lovebird does not yet exhibit the intensity of color found in adults.

Lovebirds as Tame
Household Companions?

At the end of this heading stands a question mark, because among many fanciers the opinion still prevails that young lovebirds are not inclined to be amiable and certainly not disposed to become tame pets. This is a widespread misconception. Especially Peach-faced Lovebirds and the lovebirds with white orbital rings show a definite tendency to become fully attached to people; in addition, they are considered to be the most intelligent species in the genus *Agapornis* and therefore adjust quite rapidly to life in a cage. On the other hand, it would be inexcusable to use *A. cana, A. taranta,* or possibly even *A. pullaria* for such patently selfish purposes. These species belong in flights, where they might breed and so maintain their numbers in captivity.

An important consideration for our purpose is the age of the young bird. An animal that is approximately seven weeks old and has just become independent is most suitable. One places it by itself in a large cage (about Cockatiel size; that is, at least 50 cm). The wiring of the cage must run horizontally to give the animal ample climbing opportunity. Food and water should be put in ahead of time. It is also good to scatter a handful of millet seed on the floor so that the animal quickly becomes accustomed to eating on its own. It is best to place the cage at eye level in a bright, draftfree corner. On the other hand, the kitchen and the dining room particularly are not recommended for reasons of hygiene: one should not forget that even a bird kept singly does not always sit quietly on the perch but now and then makes use of its wings and so makes some mess.

During the first two weeks, one must give his charge the opportunity to become accustomed to its new home and the surroundings. One should avoid all sudden movements and loud noises during this time so as not to frighten it, and one should speak to it only in an even, quiet voice to win its confidence. One should offer it treats through the wire (spray millet, bits of fruit), which it will soon take from the hand readily. After a time, one can try opening the cage door and carefully familiarizing the bird with one's hand. If it withdraws the first time, let it have its own way. Only when it has gotten completely used to the hand should one attempt to take it from the cage perched on a finger; while doing so, one should talk quietly to the animal. In many cases, it is by then already so confiding that it allows itself to be gently scratched and stroked. Thus the first precept in such an attempt at taming is patience; with patience, many fanciers claim, even a stubborn parrot can be transformed into a lovable household companion.

In certain cases we are acquainted with, this "love" goes so far that the animals wish to sit on the head and shoulders of the "trusted" people the entire day, if possible. Thus a tame lovebird can be simply an ideal feathered companion. It makes no great demands with respect to diet, requires little space, makes much less of a mess than larger parrots, and shows itself to have a lovable, congenial disposition.

Hence it is also evident that the widely held view that lovebirds must only be kept in pairs is erroneous. To be sure, these animals do indeed require a point of reference for a proper feeling of well-being, but this point of reference need not be a second bird exclusively; a person will also be accepted as a "mate" to which the animal will become completely attached. A requirement for keeping a lovebird singly is that one must always be personally involved with the animal, so that its disposition toward companionship will be fulfilled. Otherwise, psychological disturbances can occur and may culminate in the bird's death.

In any case, one should not make any great demands with respect to the speaking talent of these small parrots. To be sure, the literature reports on a few exceptional ones that could repeat single words or even short sentences more or less clearly, but we have not yet encountered such a bird. Of course, hand-tame lovebirds can as a rule no longer be used for breeding, since they are completely imprinted on people.

W. Kitschke of Halle told us in a letter that a tame Peach-faced Lovebird lived to an age of 17 years in captivity (kept singly). This is, by the way, the greatest age of a lovebird that we could ascertain from a poll of approximately 500 lovebird breeders (Brockmann, *AGA-Rundbriefe* 21, 1982).

Adult wild-colored (Green) Peach-faced Lovebird.

Facing page: A Masked Lovebird that has been accustomed to human contact from an early age.

A clutch of Peach-faced Lovebird eggs, which seldom amounts to more than six.

Behavior Patterns
of Lovebirds

The following discussion relies on the observations of the American ornithologist W. C. Dilger of Cornell University, Ithaca, New York, which he published in the *Zeitschrift für Tierpsychologie* in 1960.

Nestling Behavior

A few hours before hatching, one can detect the cheeping of the young bird inside the shell. At hatching, the egg breaks open at the blunt end. With powerful leg movements, the young animal frees itself from the shell completely. In no time at all, the down feathers are dry, and the young bird is fed already during the first hour by the mother. After a few days the cock also participates in feeding the young animals.

The young birds' eyes open eleven days after hatching in *A. roseicollis* and the races of *A. personata*. With *A. cana* this takes fourteen days, with *A. taranta* fifteen days. None of the *Agapornis* species show any sign of fear before the eyes open. Later, however, they all try to flee from the observer. Occasionally, young birds exhibit a tendency to bite as they approach fledging; in our experience, carefully reared animals do not bite, as a rule.

All young lovebirds have a tendency to evacuate when they are disturbed in the nest. The excreta are watery and copious.

During the nestling period the young preen themselves and one another. Often they are also assisted in this by the parents.

By the time they leave the nest, the entire plumage, except for the tail, is fully developed. Upon leaving the nest cavity they are capable of sustained flight. Their ability to maneuver is limited, but it improves after a short time. The birds stay close to the nest box for the first days, so that they can disappear back in at the slightest disturbance. Becoming used to life outside the nest progresses slowly at first. The time the young animals spend outside becomes longer and longer. Finally, one day they cease to return to the protection of the box.

Even after they leave the nest, the young birds continue to beg for food for a number of days. They utter the squeaky begging call while stretching the opened bill toward another bird. Usually the begging is directed toward the parents, but once in a while siblings or other birds in the breeding colony are solicited. Now and again it happens that one young bird feeds another.

Typical Behavior Patterns

Especially characteristic of lovebirds is the noisy behavior by which they call attention to themselves when in a flock. This loud "communication" takes place between the male and female of a pair in particular. It is most pronounced in *A. roseicollis* and in the *personata* group.

FEEDING AND DRINKING: Seeds are quickly hulled by maneuvering the kernels back and forth between the tongue and the tips of the upper and lower mandibles. The birds do not hold food in the feet, either to hull it or to carry it to the bill. In drinking, the scoop-shaped lower mandible is submerged in the water and, with a sudden, pistonlike movement of the tongue, the water is taken in.

STRETCHING MOVEMENTS: Stretching movements, which are very similar in all species of lovebirds, frequently follow a rest period. Both wings, slightly spread, may be stretched over the back simultaneously. Often, however, only one wing is extended and stretched downward. The simultaneous spreading of both wings is certainly uncommon, but, even so, it was repeatedly observed by us in the young of *A. roseicollis*.

WING FLAPPING: There is a series of actions the bird carries out to increase its well-being. Among these, wing flapping is often observed. The bird stands upright on a perch and flaps its wings forcefully. It must hold on more tightly to avoid lifting off the perch. Such exercises frequently follow a long rest, and can also often be observed in incubating females just after they leave their eggs.

PREENING: All species preen themselves as well as one another. Reciprocal preening takes place most frequently between mates and young animals that are not yet independent. It is observed less often in unpaired adults, usually among *A. roseicollis*.

Frequently, a "solicitation posture" is assumed when the head is offered for preening. The birds tilt their heads to the side, ruffle their head feathers, close the eyes completely or partly, and allow themselves to be gently preened by their neighbor. In this posture the entire plumage is often slightly fluffed as a sign of submission.

BATHING: The only kind of bathing we have been able to observe in lovebirds is bathing with water. With the exception of *A. cana* and *A. pullaria*, all species bathe in rain puddles or bath dishes. In contrast to

Peach-faced Lovebird nest containing a recently hatched chick.

Facing page: In lovebirds, reciprocal preening is part of pair bonding. The birds here are a Masked Lovebird and a Peach-faced–Masked hybrid.

Peach-faced Lovebird nestlings: Pastel-blue and Green Cinnamon.

the bathing behavior of other birds, lovebirds very rarely stand with their feet in the water. They stand on the rim of the utensil, repeatedly dipping their heads and upper bodies into the water, shaking the wings and ruffling the plumage at the same time. During a light rain, *A. cana* and *A. pullaria* were occasionally seen allowing themselves to be rained on, with ruffled feathers and their heads hanging down.

All lovebirds bathe in clean, fresh water only, but drink any water, dirty as it may be.

BILL CARE: As with many other parrots, lovebirds clean their bills by repeated wiping movements on a perch. The animals spend a large part of their time gnawing wood, as well as other things. No doubt this serves principally to abrade the bill. The steady "chewing noises" that can often be heard come from the bird rubbing the upper and lower mandibles together, which keeps the tip of the lower mandible in working order.

TAIL WAGGING: This movement—a rapid, brief vibrating of the tail—appears to enhance the bird's well-being. In the genus *Agapornis*, however, this is not part of defecation, as it is in some other birds.

RESTING AND SLEEPING: All species spend a large part of the day resting. With fully or partially closed eyes and slightly fluffed feathers, they sit quietly on a perch. Healthy animals almost always rest on one leg, with the other foot tucked in the belly feathers. Most of the species sleep by turning the head over a shoulder and burying the bill and face in the feathers of the back. They prefer to sleep on perches or on the nest-cavity floor. As when resting, the birds sit on one leg only. *A. pullaria*, exceptionally, sleeps hanging with the head down, a behavioral trait that is also known in the related parrot genus *Loriculus* (hanging-parrots). In so doing, the head is turned over the shoulder in the usual way.

Movement Sequences

All species fly swiftly and expertly and are capable of making sharp turns at high speed. Particular movements prior to flight include sleekening the plumage, crouching down, and turning the body in the intended direction of flight. Like all other parrots, lovebirds use their bill as an aid when climbing.

FIGHTING BEHAVIOR: Sleekening the plumage and the sequence of movements toward another animal indicate the impulse to attack; ruffling the feathers and movements away from another animal suggest the urge to flee. These behavioral patterns certainly function as signals that are prompted by observed behaviors. The races of the *personata* group and *A. roseicollis* exhibit an elaborate social behavior and have evolved many restraints against reciprocal biting. The biological advantage is clear in view of the powerful bills of these species.

BILL FENCING: Bill fencing appears to be a highly ritualized behavior. With lovebirds the attack is always made on the toes of the opponent and is parried with the bill. Frequently, bill fencing is only mock combat; the sudden defensive movements and attacks are apparently executed without any earnest attempt to actually bite the opponent. Even in the uncommon violent fencing between adults, serious bites occur only occasionally. A strong inhibition against biting an opponent anywhere except on the toes exists, even should such an opportunity occur in the course of fencing.

If one bird of a pair wants the other to move aside, then it will bite the other gently on the nearest toe or will make a movement as if it were going to do so. This does not result in bill fencing; the "attacked" bird then merely moves from the spot, without haste.

Actual biting attacks can be observed only in *A. cana, A. taranta,* and *A. pullaria.* Their actions appear to be less restrained. They also exhibit a wider range of gestures in their attack and escape behaviors than the more social species.

Reproduction

PAIRING: Soon after the first complete molt, the birds begin to search for mates. After they have made their choice, the birds usually remain together until the death of one of the pair. Occasionally, even young animals form pair bonds. These are as a rule heterosexual; but occasionally same-sex bonds also occur, which are not maintained after the onset of sexual maturity, however. Homosexual pair bonds have been observed only in the social species, never in *A. cana, A. taranta,* or *A. pullaria.*

In pair bonds between two birds of the same sex, one bird takes the role of the male animal and the other takes that of the female. Nevertheless, a "pair" consisting of two cocks will never use nesting material or investigate the nest box. Two females, on the other hand, will build a nest together, and both will lay eggs and incubate them.

NEST BUILDING: At the onset of sexual maturity the females immediately show a strong interest in nest holes and begin building a nest a short time later. The cocks are always found nearby, but they show more interest in the females' behavior than in nest building.

Pied Green Peach-faced Lovebird. The degree of piebaldness is extremely variable.

Facing page: A Pied Green Peach-faced Lovebird that exhibits comparatively little yellow coloration.

Pied Green Peach-faced Lovebird, a good example of a what is called "heavily pied," or "clear pied."

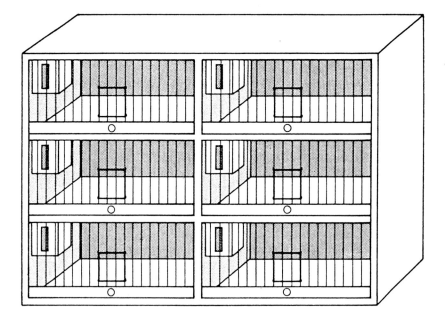

Breeding unit for lovebirds.

With the exception of *A. pullaria*, which nests in cavities excavated in termitaria or in the galleries of arboreal ants, all lovebirds use tree holes and the like as nest sites. The furnishings of the nest cavities range from the scanty nesting substrates of *A. cana* and *A. taranta* to the elaborately constructed breeding chambers made from small pieces of twigs in the most highly developed species, *A. personata*. More details on nest building can be found in the species accounts.

During the breeding season, pairs of the more primitive species—*A. cana, A. taranta,* and *A. pullaria*—separate themselves from the existing flock and go about the business of breeding. In the *personata* forms, the tendency toward communal breeding sites is already present. Finally, *A. roseicollis* is certainly a colonial nester.

SEXUAL BEHAVIOR: In general, sexual maturity occurs sooner in males than in females in all species of lovebirds. The females, on the other hand, initially react with indifference and frequently even aggressively to the cocks' courting. Gradually, though, they also display sexual behaviors, until the time comes when they can copulate successfully.

During nest building, egg laying, and the first days of incubation, the sexual behaviors of the males persist undiminished, but during the latter days of incubation they decrease, and afterwards remain weak, even during the course of a second breeding. The sexual behavior of all cocks of the genus is virtually the same.

COURTSHIP FEEDING: Courtship feeding takes place throughout the year in paired animals, increasing in frequency during the breeding season. During breeding, courtship feeding takes on added significance. The cock then supplies the female with sufficient food, as she can only leave the nest cavity a few times a day. Later, both parents take part in feeding the young animals. During this time courtship feeding occurs less often, but then increases in frequency again when the young become independent. With *A. roseicollis* and the races of *A. personata*, only the cocks feed their mates. With *A. cana* and *A. taranta*, however, reciprocal courtship feeding has frequently been observed.

COPULATION: Successful courtship by the cock culminates in the sexual act. The cock mounts the female's back. He does not fly to her, as happens with other birds. By lowering her body and spreading her wings and tail feathers slightly, the female indicates her readiness to mate. Occasionally these behavioral patterns occur during courtship by the cock, but usually only after the cock has shown the desire to mount the female. The hen rarely takes the copulatory position without preliminary activities on the part of the male.

As soon as the cock has mounted his hen, he clutches her flank feathers firmly with his feet, lowers his tail, and brings their vents into contact by forward pushing movements. Copulation consists of a series of these movements, rhythmically repeated. After mating is accomplished, the female remains in the copulatory position for another few seconds after the cock has dismounted. If insemination has taken place, the female's vent will appear swollen, moist, and reddened. Otherwise, its external appearance will be unchanged.

During treading the males seldom grasp the female's nape feathers, but they frequently use the closed bill to help them mount. The cocks also frequently extend their wings for balance. Except for *A. taranta* females, which utter soft, squeaking noises during copulation, all the others remain silent. As a rule, several mating attempts take place daily before insemination occurs. Postcopulatory behavior patterns have not yet been observed in lovebirds.

Facing page: Peach-faced Lovebirds, Blue and Pied Green.

Combining the Pied and the Blue factors produces the variety called Pied Blue (or Pied Pastel-blue), shown in these two photographs.

Breeding Lovebirds

Sexing

The breeding of lovebirds has by now been practiced for forty or fifty years, and has experienced enormous growth in the last ten years in particular. From the outset it should be said that breeding is far more easily accomplished with domesticated Budgerigars and Cockatiels than with lovebirds. Even so, certain species of these small parrots do reproduce well for experienced breeders. In theory, the fundamental requirement for success is a compatible pair. Already we have come to the primary and probably the biggest problem. If the opportunity to obtain a guaranteed breeding pair should present itself, the beginner at least should act quickly. But what breeder would sell a pair that without fault have proven themselves in rearing young?

A much more difficult course involves putting together a pair from young animals. Therefore, what follows gives the somewhat generalized sexual characteristics (of the similarly colored species): (a) In general, the females are somewhat larger than the males, and have a broader perching stance because of the wider pelvis. (b) As a rule, the male's head is flat, while that of the female has a slight arch. (c) Possibly the most important point for sexing is the spacing of the pelvic bones. However, this characteristic is useful only with mature animals. In females the space should be approximately 4–7 mm, while the cock's bones are placed very close together. The female's bones are also sturdier and more rounded, while the males have quite pointed pelvic bones. All of these characteristics admit of exceptions, however.

In order to attempt to determine a bird's sex, it is expedient to take the bird in the left hand, holding the bird's head between the thumb and index finger (to avoid bites). Now one waits a short time, until the bird lies relaxed in the hand, and then carefully probes the pelvic bones in the bird's vent area with the right index finger. If the bird's legs are folded and drawn close to the body while doing so, then the structure of the pelvic bones cannot be examined accurately and determining sex is difficult.

Lately one hears of sexing by means of endoscopy; however, this can only be done by experienced veterinarians.

Pairing

In our opinion, the best method of pairing is to leave the choice of a mate to the birds themselves. One obtains four to six birds of the same species and the same age (no siblings) and houses them together in a community cage. To be sure, with rare color varieties or species this course is hardly feasible for reasons of cost or in view of the difficulty of obtaining the necessary number of animals. The birds should be in full color, have no gaps in the plumage, and should have a notably sparkling eye and lively disposition. Avoid buying birds that are too old and unsuitable for breeding. Therefore, it is advisable to purchase only birds that have closed bands, because then you are never in the dark about the animal's age. After a short time the animals will have paired. This is indicated by perching close together regularly, particularly at dusk and at night, by reciprocal head preening, and by occasional courtship feeding. In any case, at this point it should not go unsaid that under certain conditions this behavior can also be observed with animals of the same sex. As a rule, however, such eventualities do not occur when the birds pair themselves; it mainly happens when only two birds of the same species are present.

Once the pairs have formed, the surplus animals can be removed, and one can begin with the preparations for breeding. The birds should be at least ten months old (pair bonding can also take place with considerably younger animals). During the breeding season, it is best to house each pair separately. A cage with the dimensions of 80 × 50 × 50 cm is completely adequate (see the section on accommodations).

Nest Building, Incubation, and Youngsters

Like all other parrots (with a few exceptions), lovebirds are also cavity nesters. As a substitute for trees with holes, suitable trees can be hollowed out (with difficulty, to be sure). It is easier and just as suitable to build nest boxes from wooden boards or panels. Appropriate dimensions are—for the larger species: 17 × 17 cm, and 25 cm high; for the smaller species: 15 × 17 cm, and 20 cm high.

Nest boxes can also be built according to the illustrations. It is advisable to place a ladder under the entrance hole—made of wire mesh or, better yet, from wooden slats nailed on—to make it easier for the birds

Blue (Pastel-blue) Peach-faced Lovebird. The name of this variety is troublesome to many because it is not sufficiently descriptive of the principal color.

Facing page: The Albino Peach-faced Lovebird results from a combination of the Blue and the Ino factors.

Pied Blue Peach-faced Lovebird, a nearly clear specimen.

to climb out of the box. The diameter of the entrance hole should be between 4.5 and 5.0 cm.

As nesting material, lovebirds require fresh fruit-tree twigs or, best of all, willow twigs. How the various species build their nests is mentioned in the species accounts.

Lovebird eggs are pure white and, as a rule, are laid every other day, usually in the afternoon. The clutch consists of as many as six eggs, seldom more. Although lovebirds in captivity, like Budgerigars, are not generally limited to any particular breeding season (in heated quarters they also breed in the winter), it is more promising not to begin breeding in outdoor accommodations until spring. The pairs are placed in their own breeding cages, the nest boxes are installed, and fresh willow twigs are provided. At about the same time, one should begin to stimulate the prospective parents with suitable dietary supplements (for example, egg food, sprouted seed, and a vitamin mixture).

Nest building of about ten to twenty days usually precedes the first egg laid, and is also continued during the incubation period. As a rule, the females begin incubating from the second egg on. Nevertheless, we have also had in our stocks females that sat tightly only from the third egg on. This also affects the date the young hatch. In the literature, an incubation period of approximately twenty-one days is given. However, the breeder had better count on twenty-three to twenty-five days, because there are many eventualities that may affect incubation. The young hatch according to the intervals at which the egg were laid, so that in a single nest newly hatched young as well as others with emerging feather sheaths can be found. In some cases, with too great a disparity in age, it happens that the smallest youngster is shoved aside by the older siblings during feeding, and it starves or is even crushed to death. After approximately three and a half weeks, the young have virtually complete plumage. At the age of five weeks they leave the nest, and then are still fed for another two to three weeks by their parents (particularly the cock). At this time, the female begins to renovate the nest, and a short time later lays the first egg of the next clutch. To obtain vigorous young, and also not to overstrain the parents, one should allow only two or three broods a year, and then remove the boxes.

As soon as the young have left the box, one should begin to prepare them to feed themselves by scattering some food on the floor. Sooner or later they will also begin to eat from the dishes. Approximately forty days after the last youngster hatches, the chicks may be separated from the parents. They are now able to feed themselves. After approximately six to seven months, the animals have the first molt behind them, and sex can now be determined with some degree of certainty (cocks are often in the minority). Young Black-winged Lovebirds (*A. taranta*) take longer to develop than the other species.

There are parents that will, upon beginning to nest again, violently chase their young soon after they fledge, perhaps seriously injuring them. For this reason, one should promote independent feeding in the young animals early on, and should not leave them with the parents too long, even though this appears to be going well. After the second or third brood, it is advisable to give the animals about six months of rest, to be able to start the next breeding season with rested animals. Young birds and adults should be segregated and housed outdoors until one has to transfer them to a slightly heated shelter room at the onset of winter. A certain amount of cold presents no problems for well-acclimated animals, but it is better to keep the animals warm during the winter.

Breeding Records

At this point it should perhaps be mentioned that every serious breeder should make the effort to put down in writing the exact kinship relations of the birds he rears, so as to have an accurate overview at any time. In this way, for instance, destruction of a strain through haphazard inbreeding can be avoided. A card file works well. Each breeding pair is given a record card on which ages, band numbers, and possibly also split inheritance and other peculiarities of the parents are recorded. Each breeding season will require new cards, where everything of interest concerning the breeding in a given year can be entered. In this way one always has an overview—with sequential entries—of the breeding stock, which will be of inestimable value later.

While we are still on the subject of "keeping accounts," we do not wish to neglect our duty to inform all readers that in Germany the breeding of parakeets and parrots, even if it happens to be the most insignificant Budgerigar breeding, must be licensed. It is every breeder's duty to keep a register covering the purchase, breeding, and sale of all species of parrots. In addition, the birds must be fitted with official bands. These can be obtained, for instance from the Zentralverband der Zoologischen Fachgeschäfte Deutschlands e.V. or from the Austausch-zentrale der Vogelliebhaber und -züchter e.V. These societies will ship bands only upon the submission of an official breeding permit, which is obtainable from local authorities. An authorized veterinarian will then examine the stock and assess the competence of the breeder. These regulations are designed to keep the risk of an outbreak of parrot fever (psittacosis) as small as possible.

Sundry Considerations

In breeding lovebirds the following major problems can occur. First we should consider the frequent problem of quite low hatchability. Breeders find time and again that without sufficient humidity in the nest box the hatching ratio is quite disappointing, because the embryos die inside the eggs. Frequently the young peck at the egg shell but are unable to break it open. This means that one should keep the nests moist or soak the eggs. The fact of the matter is that a certain amount of humidity appears to facilitate the hatching of the young. In the wild, where the animals live in barren, dry steppe regions, this humidity is produced by pieces of fresh tree bark. Attentive observers will have noticed that the female again and again spreads fresh pieces of bark around the eggs, even though the nest has long since been completed and all of the eggs

Yellow Peach-faced Lovebird, the result of a mutation that initially occurred in Japan.

Facing page: The Edged-yellow Peach-faced Lovebird, it seems, originated in the United States.

Another view of the Yellow Peach-faced Lovebird shown above.

have already been laid and are being incubated. There are certain measures to help nature somewhat, but one should guard against excesses, however. If the nest boxes are placed in the roofed portion of the outdoor flight, as a rule there will be no difficulties with hatching. A completely problemfree practice is to supply the birds with fresh willow twigs that are in bud. By persistently working on the nest and surrounding the clutch with pieces of bark, the females provide a constantly moist substrate within the box. It has not yet been determined if this has a detrimental effect on the business of incubating. Furthermore, a bath dish should always be available to the parents, because the animals themselves can alter too low humidity in the box by the amount of bathing, in that they sit on the eggs while wet. Of course, familiarization with bathing must have taken place long before the onset of breeding; in general, however, the animals bathe with great pleasure. A third possibility is to moisten the nest box or the nesting material once a day. Of course, caution is necessary here. The water must not be too cold, and afterward the females must return to the clutch immediately, since the eggs might otherwise cool too quickly and, at worst, the embryos might die.

In very dry indoor accommodations, besides using a humidifier, the following measure is also recommended: one makes special nest boxes. Approximately 3 cm above the floor one installs a perforated, nonrusting, thin sheet of metal, which is supported by cleats. The holes in the sheet of metal must have a very small diameter (approximately 1 mm). A small frame with mosquito netting is also suitable for this purpose. If the holes in the sheet of metal are too large, then it could happen that the tiny feet of the young birds could slip through and then they would not be able to get loose. This danger does not exist with frames of mosquito netting, but it may happen that the parents soon chew a hole in it. In the space between the floor and the netting a water dish can be placed; it should be almost flush with the mesh, if possible. On the mesh one spreads a layer of moist garden peat and then lets the birds build their own kind of nest on top of it. If the water dish is always kept filled to the rim, enough water will evaporate through the floor into the nest, so that the constant slight dampness will allow the young to hatch without much difficulty. We ourselves follow this procedure with good results.

A final and much more difficult approach is to soak the eggs. This requires considerable expertise, and we ourselves do not recommend it, since we have destroyed several clutches in this manner. It entails placing the eggs in lukewarm water—for approximately two minutes—a number of times during the second half of the incubation period. Here too the females must return to the clutch immediately after the box is hung up again!

Many well-known breeders consider that artificially increasing the humidity to facilitate hatching is wasted effort. When hatching does not seem to be very successful, then they point to low fertility or inferior breeding material. When these are not involved, it is inadequate diet, improper accommodations, or improper care. Conventional wisdom states that the animals come from very dry regions, so it is incomprehensible that they should require a certain humidity for hatching—and therefore the breeding stock is to blame.

Certainly, there are inferior breeding pairs that have the failings mentioned. As a rule, however, this is not the case with unrelated, year-old animals. In boxes that are too dry, the chicks do not hatch, even with a faultless pair and a supply of willow twigs.

When we speak of a "certain humidity," we do not mean a dripping wetness, only a slight but constant moistness within the box. Excessive humidity is not only unnecessary, but, because it fosters the growth of mold, it presents a danger to the young animals.

A second serious problem in breeding lovebirds is plucking of the young. Now and then it happens that the parents pluck the feathers of their young as they emerge. In many cases this does not cause any substantial problems in the young animals' growth, but at times the parents pluck so severely (occasionally until the young are completely bare) that one must intervene. The causes can only be discussed in quite general terms, since this problem has not been solved satisfactorily, not even by researchers.

In all likelihood, a number of factors, which must be present simultaneously, play a role in plucking. These may include boredom of the parents; very low humidity in the breeding accommodations; possibly a renewed desire to breed; and certainly an inadequate diet. We know of experiments in which lovebirds that had plucked their young were accustomed to being at liberty and afterwards once again were allowed to rear young. They were fed a varied diet; the birds themselves obtained greens, fruit, and minerals. Even so, in rearing young the signs of plucking again were noted.

As we said before, we cannot here give any definitive advice on how the animals can be cured of plucking. Fresh air, sun and rain, a varied diet, sexual maturity, breeding stock not ruined by inbreeding, and

Green Cinnamon Peach-faced Lovebird.

constantly available diversion (for example, twigs for gnawing)—these would seem to be the most important provisions against plucking. In any case, prevention is recommended here as well, because once the animals have this vice, they relinquish it only with difficulty.

64

If pluckers do happen to appear in one's stock, there are several possibilities for saving the young animals from a crippled existence or even from death. In general, it is recommended that action be taken quickly, so that the young birds are not "worked over" more than necessary by the parents. With minimal plucking, it is frequently sufficient to apply Nivea Cream thinly to the affected body part of the young bird. Sometimes the problem can be remedied in this way.

For persistent cases, there is a very practical way for saving the young. One replaces one side of the nest box with wide-mesh wire and closes off the entrance hole. At the same time one should also place several warming cloths in the nest box and, if possible, also raise the temperature in the breeding room somewhat. Lovebirds have a relatively strong feeding drive, so the parents, since they can no longer reach the young, will attempt to feed them through the mesh. After a few hours, the parents and young will understand how they must feed and be fed, respectively. In most cases there will be relatively few losses. A prerequisite is that the young should already be three to four weeks old.

To be sure, the course of development is, as a rule, disrupted somewhat, but after approximately six weeks the animals are again completely feathered and can then be released from their "prison." After only a few days the young animals will take short flights in the cage and will no longer be pestered by the parents. Once again, the cock will continue to feed until independence.

The second possibility for saving plucked young animals is this: one prescribes a "change in scenery" for the animals; that is, the young are transferred to a second nest box which is placed on the floor of the cage. In most cases the parents will continue feeding there, now without bothering the emerging feathers.

Occasionally, females abandon their clutches or broods. In this case there are also several measures that may help to save the young or the eggs. The best course is to place the eggs or young under other lovebirds (another species as well), if this arrangement can be safely and appropriately timed. In general, this is a relatively problemfree solution. If the eggs are abandoned during the incubation period, then one can even place the abandoned clutch under Budgerigars or Red-rumped Parakeets. The latter in particular have proven themselves to be outstanding foster parents. Of course, their own eggs must have been laid at approximately the same time. In addition, it is also recommended that one remove all of the eggs of the foster parents.

While rearing with Red-rumps goes relatively smoothly, the problem in using Budgerigars as foster parents is somewhat more difficult to solve. Since the newly hatched lovebirds are somewhat larger than Budgerigar nestlings, from the first day on the female Budgerigar instinctively gives them coarser food instead of the very fine pap they would otherwise be given at first. The young are unable to digest the food and so die in a short time. Therefore, some time before the hatching date one must switch the Budgerigars to easily digestible soft foods. Only when the young are several days old can one again offer a millet mixture. For this reason, it is best, if possible, to allow the young lovebirds to hatch with their own parents and to place them under the Budgerigars on the fourth or fifth day.

If one does not have the opportunity to use foster parents for rearing the young, then one can attempt the quite difficult course of hand-rearing. If the young were not fed during the first days of life, then in most cases they cannot be saved. But when the young have already reached a certain age, one can attempt to bring them through by using a liquid soft food. Although Hampe and Schwichtenberg recommend food mixtures that are laborious to prepare, today there are innumerable kinds of baby food, which need only be mixed with water or milk. One can suitably fortify this porridge with vitamin drops, mineral supplements, and cooked egg yolk. The older the animals become, the less liquid the porridge should be. Feeding is accomplished with a small spoon. After a while the young will catch on to what it's all about. This course does demand a great deal of deftness and patience from the keeper, particularly since in the beginning the young must be fed approximately every two hours. For each feeding fresh porridge must be mixed, and after the meal the animals must be carefully cleaned of all spilled food. This is not easy, but a hand-reared lovebird, like no other, is suited to being a singly kept house pet. It will be very tame and confiding, because from the beginning it is accustomed to viewing people as providers. These animals are then less suitable for breeding, however.

Unless it is absolutely necessary, re-pairing lovebirds should be avoided. If one is determined to do so, it is better if the previous mate is no longer within hearing or seeing distance, since otherwise only a very loose pair bond will develop between the new mates. This can affect breeding adversely.

The Species
of Lovebirds

Peach-faced Lovebird, *Agapornis roseicollis*

Coloration: Males and females are colored alike. The principal color of the plumage is green; head, neck, and throat pinkish red; frontal band bright red; rump light blue; bill horn color. In the young all colors paler; bill has a blackish base. *Size and weight:* Fully grown animals have a body length of approximately 17 cm. The weight is about 45 g in cocks; females are as a rule about 5 g heavier. *Eggs:* The eggs are oval and pure white. With an average size of 18 × 25 mm, they weigh approximately 3.5 g. *Subspecies:* In addition to the nominate form (*A. r. roseicollis*), there is the subspecies *A. r. catumbella*, which has a restricted range in Angola.

When Peach-faced Lovebirds were first imported in 1860 by Karl Hagenbeck, no one had the slightest suspicion of the incredible impetus these small parrots would give to the parrot fancy. As early as 1869, these birds proceeded to breed for the first time at the Berlin Aquarium, attracting attention mainly because of the manner in which they built their nest. Today, Peach-faced Lovebirds are kept by a larger number of fanciers, and the domestic demand can be satisfied by birds bred within Germany alone. Since the animals breed quite easily and prolifically, the prices have even fallen, particularly in recent years.

Sexing runs into difficulties with *A. roseicollis.* The females have a somewhat wider leg placement and are, as a rule, larger. In addition, in females the head coloration can be paler and indistinctly demarcated from the green body color. Here too the most important clue comes from palpation of the pelvic bones.

In their homeland they nest in old, rotting tree cavities or take over the abandoned nests of the Social Weaver or the Stripe-breasted Sparrow-Weaver. In captivity they readily accept ordinary wooden boxes. For nesting material the females carry pieces of peeled bark in their rump feathers into the boxes and fashion them into a cup-shaped nest. In exceptional cases the cocks also participate in nest building. The

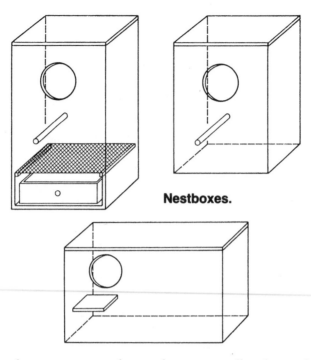

Nestboxes.

carrying of nesting material is only occasionally observed in cocks, however.

As a rule, the clutch consists of three to five eggs and is ready to hatch in approximately twenty-one to twenty-two days (if incubation begins with the first egg). The young weigh approximately 3 g at hatching, and have flesh-colored skin with orange red down. After about ten days the eyes begin to open, and the first feathers sprout. At first the color is a rather dark gray, changing to a dull green a short time later. The base of the bill is brown to blackish, the tip yellowish brown. The claws are gray. At approximately four weeks, the animals are almost completely feathered and already look out the entrance hole of the nest box. After about five weeks, the flight feathers are fully developed, and the young leave the nest box. They are readily distinguished from the parents by the dull color of the plumage and the black base of the bill. Furthermore, in many cases the sexes are most easily distinguished at this stage, because in males the frontal bands are frequently a richer red than in females, or they have a narrow red stripe over the eyes. The youngsters require two more weeks to reach independence, during which they are fed almost exclusively by the cock; then they can be separated from the parents without problems. In most cases separation from the parents is essential; otherwise, the young may sustain injuries as a result of the parents' aggressive behavior, since at this point in time the female may begin to breed again and to renovate the nest. Nevertheless, it is advisable to thoroughly clean and disinfect the nest box shortly beforehand. After approximately three months, the young birds lose the black color at the base of the bill, and after the first molt they are totally like the parents.

Peach-faced Lovebirds are considered to be the most quarrelsome members of the genus. They even bite the legs of larger birds such as Red-rumped Parakeets and Cockatiels; loss of toes is the result. One of the authors even had a pair of the exceedingly peaceful Blue-headed Parrots (*Pionus menstruus*) attacked and driven from their own territory. Similarly, when two adults were placed with a young pair six months old, one adult was killed and the other suffered extensive leg injuries. So, even young birds exhibit a pronounced drive to defend their territories. Nevertheless, colony breeding is quite possible, if all of the animals are placed in the flight at the same time and more nest boxes are always hung than the number of pairs present. A sufficiently large flight is essential. Above all, however, the nest boxes must be spaced far apart.

Lovebirds with White Orbital Rings, *Agapornis personata*

The *personata* group is divided into four subspecies, which are sufficiently diverse in coloration and size so that all four forms will be treated separately, especially since they are equally important to fanciers and breeders. Nevertheless, we agree with the many authors who treat these four forms as a single species, since behavior, nest-building practices, rearing and development of the young, and, not least, the occurrence of fertile hybrids, does not, in our estimation, allow the possibility of separating this group into four species. The lovebirds with white orbital rings build a nest from pieces of twigs. In contrast to *A. roseicollis*, they carry these into the nest box only in the bill.

Masked Lovebird, *A. p. personata*. *Coloration:* Males and females colored alike. The principal color of the plumage is green; head brownish black to black; nape, throat, and breast region bright yellow; rump watery blue; bill red; white orbital ring. In the young all colors are paler; bill has black base; head brownish; breast region murky yellow. *Size and weight:* The size of the animals is approximately 16 cm. Fully grown cocks weigh approximately 48 g, females about 55 g. *Eggs:* The eggs are pure white and have a weight of approximately 3.8 g and average 18 × 24 mm.

The Masked Lovebird, along with the Peach-faced and the Fischer's lovebirds, are among the most popular and most numerous species in fanciers' aviaries. Breeding is not always as easy as with the Peach-faced Lovebird, and complications often occur. For this reason, prices stay relatively constant. If one compares the advertisement sections in specialty journals from 1980 with those from 1960, one can see that Masked Lovebirds are still at the same price level. The reasons for this can certainly lie in the breeding problems just mentioned.

In fully colored Masked Lovebirds the sexes are somewhat easier to distinguish than with the previously discussed species. In addition to the general sexual characteristics, the breeder can also distinguish the sexes by certain external characteristics of this form. So, for example, the white orbital ring is somewhat wider and has an oval shape in the female. The male's orbital ring is in most cases more rounded. In mature (fully colored) animals head color also plays a role: the cock has a very dark, almost black, head color, while that of the female is more likely blackish brown. Frequently, with females the color of the head is only indistinctly set off from the yellow breast region, while many cocks exhibit a clear, sharp separation of colors. Also, we have often had the impression that in the Masked Lovebird considerable differences between the sexes with respect to body size can also be noted.

Masked Lovebirds too should be set up for breeding only when they are approximately ten months old. Although with many species of parrots it is of paramount importance that mates be compatible, with the domesticated species of lovebirds it often happens that two birds randomly "thrown together" form a pair bond. Nest building basically proceeds just as it does in the Peach-faced Lovebird. The animals peel relatively long and wide pieces of bark from branches and use them to build a rough, bulky nest cup. The entire nest box is filled with material; a fist-sized hollow in the middle, furnished with very fine building materials (fine twigs, small pieces of bark, feathers), remains to serve as the future nursery. The cock eagerly takes part in the nest building too and later occasionally helps with incubation.

Shortly before the first egg is laid, the female's droppings become more watery and increase in volume. The egg by then is also evident in the female's lower belly, so that one can roughly estimate the time of laying. In the nest hollow described, the female lays between three and six eggs, usually five, which will hatch in approximately twenty-two days.

During the incubation period the female leaves the nest box only to eat and to evacuate. Frequently the cock feeds the female inside the nest box or at the entrance hole. In most cases the male stands guard at the entrance hole or conceals himself in the nest box between the roof and the nest. At any sign of danger the cock gives his special, quickly repeated alarm call and disappears into the nest box.

If both animals find themselves out of the box and wish to return to it, then they always do so in a particular order. Even when they are very frightened, the female always retreats into the box first, and only then does the cock follow. Leaving the nest takes place in reverse order.

The newly hatched young are just like those of the Peach-faced Lovebird. Soon they show the first yellow and black feathers. The young are fully feathered at an age of three and a half to four weeks and leave the box after approximately thirty-five days. At seven weeks the young can be transferred to separate cages without worry.

Since the nest cup becomes thoroughly flattened down during the development of the young, after they fledge the female begins at once to rebuild the nest with new material. However, for reasons of hygiene, it is better to remove the old material and thoroughly clean the box. Only then should one allow a second brood. It occasionally happens that eggs are already in the box before the last young bird has fledged. It can happen that the female will drive this young bird out and, worst of all, injure it or even kill it.

Occasionally, young Masked Lovebirds have deep yellow to orange-red feathers at the base of the neck, which they usually lose after the first molt. It is claimed that Masked Lovebirds that are split for Yellow have this color on the breast. With us, however, young of this kind come from pure Green parents. It is also possible that such an appearance is the result of earlier crosses with *A. p. fischeri*, though we have also observed the same coloration in birds imported from Africa (Brockmann 1984).

Hybridization with Fischer's, Nyasa, and Black-cheeked lovebirds is not difficult. Crossing Masked Lovebird × Peach-faced Lovebird has also been accomplished, but in our experience the offspring are sterile.

Fischer's Lovebird, *A. p. fischeri*. *Coloration:* Males and females are alike in color. The principal color of the plumage is green; forehead, cheeks, and throat orange red, occiput brownish yellow; nape yellow; breast region orange yellow; rump feathers watery blue; bill red; orbital ring white. In the young all colors are paler. *Size and weight:* The body length of mature animals is approximately 15 cm. Their weight is approximately 43 g, and here too the females weigh about 5 g more. *Eggs:* The oval eggs weigh approximately 3.3 g and are approximately 22 × 17 mm in size.

Although Fischer's Lovebirds are among the more easily bred species, the demand for them has decreased; thus, unfortunately, they are, if not rare, certainly uncommon among fanciers. The reason for this, in part, is that there are few color varieties in this subspecies, compared with Masked and Peach-faced lovebirds. With respect to price, the animals are at about the same level as *A. p. personata.*

With Fischer's Lovebirds it is quite difficult to distinguish the sexes. The difference in size between males and females is, however, more distinct than in the other forms. In addition, the cock's head appears small and narrow when viewed from the front. Here too, the surest characteristics are behavior and the spacing of the pelvic bones.

Like Masked Lovebirds, these animals must be approximately ten months old before one can use them for breeding. A compatible pair is the best prerequisite for success. The ideal breeding time is spring or early summer. One should not, however, put the birds in flights outdoors too early. The cock initiates courtship by feeding the female, always regurgitating the food with the usual nodding head movements. Then, at irregular intervals, the peculiar head scratching ("from behind"), which is observed in the cock in particular, follows. This characteristic often serves to distinguish the sexes, because females, as a rule, do not scratch themselves as frequently. The entire performance is accompanied by bill clicking (only in the cock). After a few minutes the male then awkwardly attempts to step onto the female (instead of flying to her). Frequently, a number of attempts are necessary before the cock succeeds. Copulation frequently takes place very quickly; occasionally it only lasts a few seconds. Other authors speak of several minutes, but we have not yet observed this.

Nest building proceeds in the same fashion as with the Masked Lovebird. Incubation and the development of the young are also almost identical. An astounding amount of nesting material must be supplied to the animals before they have completed a nest suitable for a single brood. Therefore one should always have fresh twigs on hand. It is best to stand them in a bucket of water, so that they do not dry out; they will even develop roots. If the need is great, it is advisable to plant one's own willows early, to be able to "harvest" them later. If one needs only a small amount, then one can use willows growing wild. But beware: willows are protected [in Germany]. Besides, shrubs growing along roads are often polluted.

As a rule, Fischer's Lovebirds are somewhat more sociable than Masked Lovebirds and therefore are considerably easier to keep and breed in colonies.

One frequently sees animals with washed-out colors, which can be traced back to crosses with other species. The breeder should therefore put a high value on clear, clean colors to achieve a pure strain. Crosses with Black-cheeked, Masked, and Nyasa lovebirds succeed without difficulty. The most attractive birds come from the pairing *A. p. personata* × *A. p. fischeri*. Nevertheless, such crosses are not recommended because, in the long run, they result in undefinable hybrids. Moreover, it is irresponsible to endanger or even to ruin pure *Agapornis* stock through constantly breeding hybrids. Amazingly, Fischer's Lovebirds are more inclined than other *Agapornis* forms to pluck their nestlings.

Black-cheeked Lovebird, *A. p. nigrigenis*. *Coloration:* Males and females are alike in color. The principal color of the plumage is green; head dark brown; nape and sides of neck yellowish brown, throat orangish brown; bill red; white orbital ring. In the young all colors are duller. *Size and weight:* These animals are approximately 14–15 cm long and weigh between 36 and 48 g. In the Black-cheeked Lovebird as well, the females are heavier. *Eggs:* The eggs are 22 × 17 mm, weighing about 3.3 g.

Black-cheeked Lovebirds are frequently described as good breeders, as lovebirds go. Here too, the greatest difficulty is distinguishing the sexes. Usually the animals can only be sexed by their behavior.

In earlier days, Black-cheeked Lovebirds were imported in large numbers, but today it is quite difficult to obtain pure animals. Along with the Nyasa Lovebird (*A. p. lilianae*) and the Red-faced Lovebird (*A. pullaria*), they are the most expensive lovebirds.

A. p. nigrigenis are quite peaceful among themselves and toward other parrots. Their vocalizations are not as penetrating as those of Masked Lovebirds.

In courtship, incubation behavior, rearing, and development of young, they are just like the Masked Lovebird and therefore do not need to be treated separately.

It is certainly astounding that this species for the most part is absent from the aviaries of German fanciers, particularly since in the past they were imported in large numbers. Unfortunately, in those days they were often mated with Masked Lovebirds.

Pure Black-cheeked Lovebirds must have neither black heads nor yellow on the breast, and the rump feathers must not be blue either. Thus special thanks must go to the few fanciers who painstakingly try to build up pure *nigrigenis* stocks. It would be a shame if we are unable to maintain this subspecies, since one can hardly count on importation, in view of the current export bans.

Nyasa Lovebird, A. p. lilianae. *Coloration:* Males and females are alike in color. The principal color of the plumage is green; front of head and throat orangish red; nape olive green, rump feathers green; bill red; orbital ring white. In the young all colors are duller; dark cheeks. *Size and weight:* Fully grown Nyasa Lovebirds are approximately 14 cm long. They reach a weight of approximately 40 g; the females are slightly heavier. *Eggs:* Pure white, with an average size of 17 × 21 mm, approximately 3.2 g in weight.

The Nyasa Lovebird is frequently confused with Fischer's Lovebird, but there are several reliable characteristics for distinguishing between these two species. First of all, Nyasa Lovebirds are somewhat smaller than *A. p. fischeri*. Furthermore, pure animals have no blue rump feathers. Even a slight amount of blue color indicates prior crossing with Fischer's Lovebirds. The facial mask of the Nyasa Lovebird is quite clearly different from that of Fischer's Lovebird. In the former, the orangish red head color is quite distinctly set off from the olive green of the nape region, while in *A. p. fischeri* the colors intermingle more. In addition, the frontal region is not as bright a red in Fischer's Lovebird.

This subspecies is also rare in the trade, but still somewhat easier to find than the Black-cheeked and Red-faced lovebirds. In price, it is on a level with *A. p. nigrigenis*.

It is somewhat more difficult to breed the Nyasa Lovebird than the other lovebirds of the *personata* group. These small parrots soon show themselves to be ready to breed, but the mortality rate of youngsters and adults is also high. If possible, one should not purchase young animals that have just become independent, but instead choose ones that have already completely finished the molt.

As the sexes are very difficult to distinguish, this is best done by behavior. The external characteristics, including sexing on the basis of the pelvic bones, do not always give an accurate determination.

In the last two years, Nyasa Lovebirds have occasionally been offered, at high prices. A number of new imports are said to have entered
in 1978, although several African countries have instituted export em-
bargos. The majority of these animals went to well-known breeders in
the Münster region. However, only a few of these birds could be kept
alive and brought to breed.

This species will probably never become common, although one
must expect that in the near future the number bred in captivity will
at least increase, and Nyasa Lovebirds will then become more affordable for some fanciers.

Black-winged Lovebird, *Agapornis taranta*

Coloration: In males the principal color of the plumage is green; forehead and bill red; underwing coverts black. Females are colored like
males but with no red on the head and brown underwing coverts. In
the young all colors are paler; bill yellowish brown. The first red feathers of males appear after three or four months. *Size and weight:* The
average size of fully grown cocks is about 16 cm, weighing 65 g. The
females are usually substantially smaller and weigh approximately 8–10
g less. *Eggs:* Oval and pure white, with a size of 25 × 19 mm, and
weighing approximately 4.5 g. *Subspecies:* Besides the nominate form,
the race *A. t. nana*, which was described in 1934 by Neumann, is also
recognized. This subspecies is markedly smaller. Black-winged Lovebirds are among the more difficult-to-breed *Agapornis* species. Because
of their quite monotonous coloration they lag behind the other species
in popularity.

Black-winged Lovebirds have never been common in the bird trade;
they have always been imported only in small numbers. Even in recent
times, because of wars in their homeland, no new imports to the German Federal Republic have taken place, so that one rarely encounters
these animals in the hands of fanciers.

Nevertheless, when they occasionally do appear for sale, they are always affordable; their price is about twice that of the Masked Lovebird.
A. t. taranta is not as easily bred as the previously described species.
On the other hand, the sexes are easy to distinguish. With young animals that are not fully colored, one can pull a few small feathers out of
the forehead region. If they grow back red, then the bird is a cock.

In their homeland, Black-winged Lovebirds are found up to altitudes
of 3000 m. Therefore, even severe cold has little effect on them, and

they can be wintered in unheated, but dry and draftfree, shelter rooms. In contrast to the species discussed so far, they do not build a covered nest, but always build a nesting substrate of bits of leaves (ivy or other evergreen plants). They frequently nest on the bare wood as well; therefore, a concavity should be made in the nest-box floor, so the eggs do not roll around.

Breeding begins in early spring (February). The clutch consists of two to five eggs, and, as a rule, is incubated for twenty-four or twenty-five days. After approximately thirty days the young are fully feathered. After six weeks they leave the nest, but the parents continue to care for them for some time. The youngsters resemble the female, but their bills are still colored yellowish brown. After about three months, they begin to molt and are in full color at about ten months.

During the breeding season, Black-winged Lovebirds are relatively unsociable and are best kept pairwise. Although breeding has been successful in the usual box cages, it is better to house them in small aviaries outdoors. In general, the animals are not bothered by nest-box inspections. The Black-winged Lovebird's voice is quiet chirping that is considered to be much less unpleasant than is often the case with other *Agapornis* species.

Grey-headed Lovebird, *Agapornis cana*

Coloration: Males are green, with the head to base of breast light gray. Females are green overall, the head somewhat darker. In the young all colors are duller. Imported young males are uniformly green; in domestically bred males the head and breast region are a medium gray that changes to a lighter color after the molt. *Size and weight:* With a length of 13 cm the Grey-headed Lovebird is one of the smallest lovebirds. Males and females are about the same size and have the same weight: about 25 g. *Eggs:* Roundish, about 17 × 19 mm, weighing approximately 3 g. *Subspecies:* Besides the nominate form, the subspecies A. c. ablectanea described by Bangs is also recognized.

Housing in a large outdoor aviary is not recommended for *A. cana,* since they would stay very shy there. A small indoor flight or a large box cage closed on three sides would be ideal accommodations. The Grey-headed and Red-faced lovebirds are among the most primitive species of their genus (Dilger 1960). They lack the ability to become closely attached to people. For this reason, in captivity they almost always remain quite shy and unapproachable. In the long run, only young birds become tame.

In addition, this species is not so easily bred, compared to other species of lovebirds. Certainly this is due in part to the shyness of these animals. Ever since an export embargo was instituted on Madagascar, Grey-headed Lovebirds become available here only in roundabout ways and in small numbers. For a long time, the demand has not been satisfied by birds bred in Germany; but then, Grey-headed Lovebirds have never been particularly prized. This probably has something to do with the difficulties in propagating them and with their plain appearance. In price, they are on about the same level as the *taranta* lovebirds.

Breeding takes much the same course as it does with the Peach-faced Lovebird, but one must reckon with many difficulties from the start, since the animals are sensitive to disturbances of all kinds (particularly to nest-box inspections). When one approaches the cage they disappear into the nest box with a great hue and cry.

This species readily accepts a normal Budgerigar nest box for breeding. Since Grey-headed Lovebirds generally use little or no nesting material, the floor of the nest box must have a concavity. Yet it has also happened that the birds have built substantial nests. The various nesting materials (principally pieces of rhododendron leaves) are carried to the nest in the back feathers (Brockmann 1983c). The clutch usually consists of four eggs which are incubated for twenty-one to twenty-two days. After leaving the nest, the young birds are cared for principally by the cock, while the female renovates the nest for another brood. De Grahl (1969) recommends sprouted millet spray as a rearing food.

In captivity, no juvenile molt takes place (as also happens with several other species of birds). Therefore, cocks bred in captivity have a silver gray head from the start, while in the wild both sexes resemble the adult female until the first molt. All in all, Grey-headed Lovebirds should be purchased by experienced parrot fanciers only, since they are certainly much more difficult to keep and breed than the other species. Beginners should confine themselves to the commonly bred lovebirds. Imports must be wintered at 10 C. at least. Birds bred in captivity can withstand temperatures near freezing if housed in dry, draftfree places.

Black-collared Lovebird, *Agapornis swinderniana*

Coloration: Males and females alike in color. The principal plumage color is green; breast olive yellow; nape band black; upper tail coverts blue; base of tail red; bill black; iris orangish yellow. In the young all colors are paler, with no black nape band and a lighter bill. *Size and weight:* The length is approximately 13 cm, the weight about 35 g.

Eggs: No details are known about the shape, weight, and size of the eggs. *Subspecies:* besides the nominate form, there are two subspecies: *A. s. zenkeri* has a brownish red neck band below the black one. It occurs in central Africa. *A. s. emini* is very similar to *A. s. zenkeri* but has a less intensely colored neck band (Forshaw).

So far this *Agapornis* species has had no significance for us fanciers, because only recently has it been possible to bring them to Europe alive. The imported birds did not survive the quarantine period, however.

According to various ornithologists, there are two reasons that contribute to the fact that these animals have rarely been imported to Europe in the past. According to Forshaw, Prof. Stresemann maintains that since the Black-collared Lovebird is a thoroughly arboreal bird, it is never found on the ground and so cannot be captured. In contrast to other *Agapornis* species, they are said to stay in the crowns of tall primary-forest trees constantly. The second, and apparently more important reason, is the difficulty of feeding this bird; various researchers say that they eat only a particular kind of fig. On the other hand, Forshaw reports that in another locality they come to the ground to feed on farm-land grain. As secondary foods he names insects and maize (milk-ripe); both were found in the crops of Black-collared Lovebirds upon dissection. Nevertheless, in the Congo Père Hutsebout was not able to keep Black-collared Lovebirds alive on substitute foods (Forshaw). Without the right figs they perished after three to four days.

The breeding season is said to occur in July (Forshaw 1973). They breed in the nests of arboreal termites (Bouet 1961), as do Red-faced Lovebirds, or in the usual tree holes (Delpy & Bischoff 1982).

Red-faced Lovebird, *Agapornis pullaria*

Coloration: In males the principal color of the plumage is green; forehead, sides of head and base of throat orangish red; rump blue; underwing feathers black; bill red. Females have a paler red and the head, underwing feathers green. The young are duller in colors. *Size and weight:* size about 14 cm, weight approximately 40 g. *Eggs:* the size of the eggs is approximately 17 × 21 mm, with a weight of 4 g. *Subspecies: A. p. ugandae* was described as a subspecies by Von Neumann.

After the last World War, large importations of this species were made into Germany, and the animals could be purchased at favorable prices. Today, Red-faced Lovebirds can be obtained only exceptionally, and one must reckon with a very high price.

In their homeland, these lovebirds nest in termitaria and the nests of arboreal ants (Dilger 1960). In these the females excavate their nest cavities and, as a rule lay between five and seven eggs, which are incubated for approximately twenty-two days.

Since Red-faced Lovebirds, along with the Grey-headed and Black-winged lovebirds, are one of the more primitive *Agapornis* species (Dilger 1960), their inability to adapt makes it difficult for them to adjust to the nesting conditions usual in captivity. For this reason, breeding has seldom been completely successful. To be sure, they have bred in ordinary wooden nest boxes, but, as a rule, the breeder must think of other possibilities to induce them to breed. Some have tried tamping moist peat into wooden boxes, to allow the females to construct passages and cavities in it. But often the passages or cavities caved in, and the females, along with their eggs or young, were buried under heaps of peat.

Hampe put a large mound of clay in an aviary, and the females constructed passages with fist-sized cavities at the ends. After many days, when he no longer expected a successful breeding, a fully feathered young bird appeared at the cavity entrance; however, it died before the first molt after a drop in temperature.

In another attempt, large blocks of cork were put up the trees, and after these were equipped with landing perches, the animals began to excavate. But in this case as well, the attempt was not fully successful.

Complete success was had by Zürcher of Ostermunding. After many disappointing attempts (infertile eggs, dead embryos, unfed young), several young Red-faced Lovebirds were reared in the autumn of 1976. He too had packed moist peat into large wooden nest boxes, for the female to construct a nest cavity.

Whoever has the great fortune to own animals of this species should never take risks of any kind. Imports as well as young animals must be wintered in dry and draftfree quarters at temperatures above 15 C.

Animals bred in captivity are easier to convert to normal wooden nest boxes. Also, such animals, once they have molted, are also less sensitive to the bad weather of our area. In any case, it is high time that fanciers of this species find ways to breed these animals more easily. Otherwise, Red-faced Lovebirds will disappear from Europe in a few years, since importation from their homeland can no longer be counted on.

Color Varieties and Their Inheritance

Peach-faced Lovebird, *A. roseicollis*

Wild-colored (Green) Peach-faced Lovebirds. The Peach-faced are certainly the lovebirds most frequently encountered in captivity. This is because they are relatively easy to breed; thus a fancier does not keep these birds only "to look at" but can also have the experience of successful breeding. Anyone who wishes to build up a stock of lovebirds should begin with the Peach-faced Lovebird, in order to gain experience with this genus without having to go through many disappointments.

Since, as a rule, Peach-faced Lovebirds reward us with numerous progeny when kept correctly, the color mutations that occur now and then can be noticed and retained.

Before we describe the different color varieties and combinations in greater detail, we will first provide some background on the coloration of wild Peach-faced Lovebirds. The ground color is green, which every breeder of course knows. As simple as this is to ascertain, in actuality the situation is somewhat more complicated. In 1929, Duncker reported the results of his research into the inherited color traits in Budgerigars (in *Kurzgefassten Vererbungslehre für Kleinvogelzüchter*). His conclusions are still recognized as valid by Budgerigar breeders and are taken into consideration in all careful color breeding. In recent years it has become clear that the color mutations which in the meanwhile have appeared in Peach-faced Lovebirds are inherited in the same or in a similar fashion as the colors of the Budgerigar. For this reason, one can safely proceed on the notion that the ground color of the feathers of the Peach-faced Lovebird has the same composition as that found in the Budgerigar (this is also true for the other species of lovebirds). Duncker and others have analyzed these feathers closely, even microscopically. The result, bewildering to many breeders, is this: there is no green pigmentation in the Budgerigar. Therefore, it is certain that green pigmentation is lacking in the Peach-faced Lovebird's plumage as well. Although the Peach-faced Lovebird is clearly green, this green is nevertheless not present as an actual pigment; instead, it arises from a mixture of yellow and blue. This will be easy to understand if one examines the structure of a feather under a microscope.

On the macro level we notice that a not particularly specialized contour feather is composed of vanes (vexillum) and the stiffer longitudinal axis, the feather 'keel' (scapus). On the feather keel one distinguishes the quill, which is free of vanes and is partially imbedded in the skin. The part of the feather keel that carries the vanes is called the feather shaft (rachis). The vane is made up of feather barbs (rami), which stand out from the feather shaft at a sharp angle. These feather barbs in turn carry barbules (radii), which are differently constructed on their two sides. Those barbules pointing toward the tip of the feather are equipped with hooklets (hamuli, or radioli) and so can anchor themselves on those barbules of the adjacent feather barb that points toward the quill, which have a flange and groove.

If one prepares a section of a barb from a green Budgerigar feather— or a Peach-faced Lovebird feather—and places it under a microscope, then one can clearly distinguish different layers.

On the outside, one can recognize a more or less amorphous, yellow-colored layer, which is called the cortex. The yellow coloration of this keratinous layer is caused by the pigment it contains, the psittacin. This pigment cannot be synthesized by the bird itself, but instead is obtained from the food and transported to the developing feathers by the blood. The pigment is incorporated in the keratin of the feather during the keratinization process. Therefore, deposition of psittacin is possible only during a feather's growth; no more pigment can be incorporated later. This is a phenomenon which is well known to all canary breeders, for instance.

In the microscope image one can also observe that a cell layer is located beneath the cortex. Each of these cells are traversed by a network of vacuoles, with a large hollow space in the middle. The cell walls are thickened. These unpigmented cells are called cloudy cells.

In the center of the barb is the medulla, of which the individual cells, barely distinguishable under the microscope, are filled with large numbers of dark pigment granules (melanins). These melanin granules come from the body's own protein production and are deposited in the shaft, barbs, and barbules during feather growth.

The reader will now ask himself where the blue color mentioned above happens to be concealed. This blue cannot be found under the microscope; there is no further color in the feather besides the psittacin in the cortex. What is involved here is not an actual color, but a structural color, which is produced by optical processes.

Such a structural color is also shown by, for example, the sky, which, everyone knows, contains no blue pigment. The extremely fine dust particles in the air scatter the blue component of sunlight more than the other colors of the spectrum. However, this becomes visible to us only against a black background, which in this case is the darkness of space. There are many other examples of optical phenomena of this kind. Thus a drop of milk on a black plate appears blue to our eyes, because the small particles in the milk reflect only the blue light. We see a similar phenomenon when we view cigarette smoke in front of a dark background.

In the feathers of Peach-faced Lovebirds, this dark background is provided by the melanin present in the medulla; the refractive in front of this background is composed of the cloudy cells with their minute, gas-filled vacuoles.

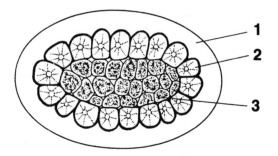

Simplified cross-section of a feather barb:
1, cortex;
2, cloudy cells;
3, medulla.

In summary one must therefore say: In a Peach-faced Lovebird's feather we find a yellow pigment and the blue structural color. Together these cause the feather to appear green! The color green is therefore not a single characteristic, but instead is made up of the characteristics yellow and blue. This must be considered carefully in any analysis of color inheritance.

But first let us consider some fundamentals to better understand genetic processes. Each animal species has in each of its living somatic cells a species-characteristic number of chromosomes, which Correns recognized as vehicles of genetic material as early as 1900. Then, in 1903, the German Boveri and the American Sutton proposed the chromosome theory, which states that the chromosomes are the carriers of the genetic factors. In each of the birds' somatic cells the chromosomes occur in pairs (autosomes) and in their entirety constitute a double set (diploid chromosome set). The chromosomes responsible for determining sex, the sex chromosomes (gonosomes, or heterosomes) present an exception which will be discussed later.

When a somatic cell divides, the chromosomes split apart longitudinally, and each new somatic cell receives one part (chromatid). The chromatids finally duplicate themselves exactly again. This process (mitosis) takes place at each further cell division; it ensures that each somatic cell receives identical genetic factors, since the chromosomes are, after all, the carriers of these factors.

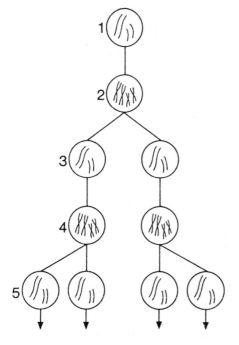

Representation of the stages in the mitotic division of somatic cells (highly simplified—only two chromosome pairs are shown).
1 – Somatic cell with diploid chromosome set.
2 – The chromosomes split apart lengthwise.
3 – Two new somatic cells having the same chromosome sets are produced.
4 – The chromatids duplicate themselves exactly.
5 – Four somatic cells with the same chromosome sets are produced. And so forth.

It is different with the male and female gametes (sperm and egg cells). It logically follows that they must not have the diploid chromosome set. If such diploid cells should happen to combine with each other at fertilization, then the new cell (zygote), and therefore also the offspring, would have a double chromosome set, compared to their parents. In each succeeding generation the chromosome set would again double—ad infinitum.

The diploid gametocytes, which are present in large numbers in the testicles or ovaries, therefore undergo other divisions before the gametes are formed. Very greatly simplified, this can be represented visually, in the accompanying diagram.

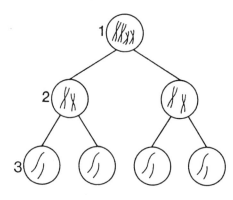

1 – The gametocyte has a diploid chromosome set. Each of the chromosomes consists of two chromatids.
2 – The first division (meiosis) produces two new cells, which possess a haploid chromosome set, as each contains one member of each chromosome pair.
3 – A second division occurs, in which each chromosome splits longitudinally into two chromatids. This results in four gametes, which are haploid. The chromatids replicate themselves exactly, so that the chromosomes are reconstituted completely.

From one gametocyte four gametes have been formed, which now have only a haploid chromosome set. In principle, both sperm cells and egg cells are formed in the same way. In male animals, four sperm cells result from the process. In females, however, the gametocyte splits off only a small cell (polar body) with a haploid chromosome set in the first meiotic division. In the second division this process is repeated, and the first polar body also simultaneously divides. Thus, in the female four cells do develop from one gametocyte as well; however, only one becomes a fertile egg cell, while the remainder (polar bodies) wither away.

Through the meiotic divisions, each gamete that is formed receives a haploid but complete chromosome set (N). At fertilization, sperm and egg cells come together, and thus the fertilized egg cell again has the diploid chromosome set (2N), that is, the set that is characteristic of this species of animal. Each chromosome pair consists of one homologue received from the mother and one from the father. Through repeated divisions of the fertilized egg cell (mitosis), the new organism develops.

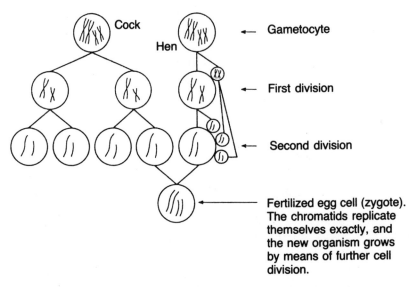

— Gametocyte

— First division

— Second division

← Fertilized egg cell (zygote). The chromatids replicate themselves exactly, and the new organism grows by means of further cell division.

At the first meiotic division, the homologues of each pair are assorted into the gametes independently of other pairs, in free combination. This should be made clear by an additional sketch.

Gametocyte: three pairs of chromosomes are shown, marked A–a, B–b, and C–c.

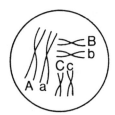

In this example, an animal having three chromosome pairs, all gametocytes would have equivalent chromosome sets. Thus any given gamete would contain one of the following possible combinations:

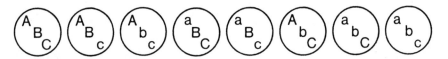

The more chromosomes a particular animal species has, the greater the number of possible combinations. Thus, for example, people have a diploid chromosome set of 46, the pigeon 16, the earthworm 32, the domestic cat 38, the gorilla 48, the cow 60, the chicken 78, *Eupagurus ochotensis* (a crab) 254, and *Ophioglossum vulgatum* (a fern) 500. Although the chromosome sets in the somatic cells of many organisms have been studied in recent years, we were, unfortunately, unable to find any data concerning the chromosome number of the various love-bird species.

Let us now turn to the heredity of the green ground color in the Peach-faced Lovebird. It should be recalled that the green is made up of a yellow pigment and the blue structural color. Utterly simplified, one can represent it this way:

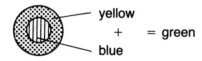

These two colors are transmitted genetically by at least one factor each (exceptions will be discussed later with the inheritance of the Ino factor, the Dark factor, etc.). Since factors for the same characteristics of the organism lie on each homologue of a chromosome pair, and since diploid chromosome sets are present in the somatic cells and also in the gametocytes, the genes for yellow and blue must therefore each be present twice in these cells.

We wish to introduce the following symbols for these factors:

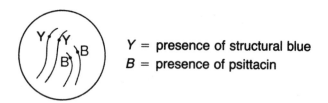

Y = presence of structural blue
B = presence of psittacin

We must suppose that the two genes (Y and B) lie on different chromosomes; this is supported by all the data on color breeding in the Peach-faced Lovebird. For the sake of simplicity, only the two chromosome pairs on which Y and B are presumed to lie have been illustrated in the sketch. As the chromosomes duplicate themselves identically, then the genes for the presence of yellow or blue coloration of course lie on each of the chromatids. Therefore, if we cross a pure Green male (the breeder uses the symbol 1,0 for him, as we also wish to do from now on) with a pure Green female (0,1), then the following picture results:

86

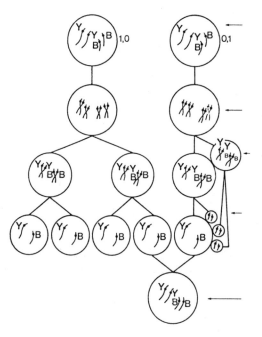

Somatic cell with diploid chromosome set (only one chromatid is shown).

Somatic cell or gametocyte with exactly duplicated chromatids.

First division: only a haploid chromosome set is present.

Second division: each gamete possesses only one factor for yellow and one for blue.

The fertilized egg cell (zygote) again possesses two factors for yellow and for blue.

Through cell division, a new Peach-faced Lovebird again develops from the fertilized egg cell. It has inherited the factors for a yellow cortex and for the blue structural color from its parents. Since the homologous chromosomes, which carry either the factors Y and B, are always separated at the first meiotic division, then each gamete must receive one of each of these genes.

In diagramming inheritance, we wish to dispense with representation of the chromosomes as much as possible, since we know from experience that otherwise many breeders would skip this chapter, unfortunately, because they think that it is all much too complicated. Nevertheless, anyone who wishes to engage seriously in the color breeding of the Peach-faced or other lovebirds must at least familiarize himself with the fundamentals of heredity, for two reasons: (1) Through accurate records the breeder can keep track of the inheritance of the different colors, making the correct pairings to achieve the desired result. (2) The lovebird fancier cannot be so easily deceived by unscrupulous breeders if he himself understands something about color inheritance.

Simplified, then, the inheritance of the Green variety can be represented in the following diagram, where B is the factor producing psittacin and Y is responsible for structural blue:

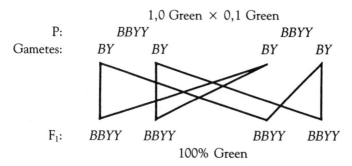

1,0 Green × 0,1 Green

| P: | BBYY | | | BBYY | |
| Gametes: | BY | BY | | BY | BY |

| F₁: | BBYY | BBYY | | BBYY | BBYY |

100% Green

Blue Peach-faced Lovebirds. Blue Peach-faced Lovebirds are today, apart from the Green, probably the best known Peach-faced Lovebird of all. They are said to have first occurred out of a normal (Green) pair owned by P. Habets in the Netherlands in 1963 (some authors also cite Weber, in Switzerland, in 1967).

Blue Peach-faced Lovebirds do not in any real sense exhibit a true blue, but instead are the color of green and blue mixed, which many breeders call Pastel-blue or Mignonette-blue. The forehead is pinkish red, the cheeks and the throat are light gray with a light pink tinge. The colors of the rump, legs, toes, and claws are the same as those of the wild bird.

How can such a Blue Peach-faced Lovebird occur? Let us recall that the green color in the wild bird is produced by the presence of yellow and blue. If then the feather is to be blue, the yellow must disappear from the cortex. Examinations of Budgerigar feathers have shown that this actually is the case. The structure of the cloudy cells and the deposit of melanin in the medulla are retained, however. Thus, the bird appears blue to our eyes, although the feathers have no pigmentation at all.

This is explicable only when we assume that the factors producing yellow have changed into factors for a lack of yellow. One calls this a mutation. Since only the factor (gene) for the color has mutated, one speaks of a gene mutation. (There can also be a change in the structure of individual chromosomes, or chromosome mutations, as well as a change in the number of chromosomes, or genome mutation.) Such mutations occur accidentally and randomly. One cannot predict which factors will mutate or when they will mutate. However, mutations are inheritable if they appear in the gametes (and also in the gametocytes). The inheritance involved in crossing a pure Green with a pure Blue Peach-faced Lovebird will now be explained.

The two birds will have feathers that in cross-section (simplified) look like this:

The green bird therefore has two factors for the production of yellow as well as two for blue, while the Blue bird has two for a lack of yellow along with two that produce blue.

We again choose letters as symbols for the factors: B = factor that produces yellow coloration (nonBlue); b = factor for a lack of yellow (produces the variety called Blue); Y = factor that produces structural-blue coloration. The genetic makeup, or genotypes, of the birds therefore look like this: Green: $BBYY$; Blue: $bbYY$. Using the diagram already employed, the following picture results:

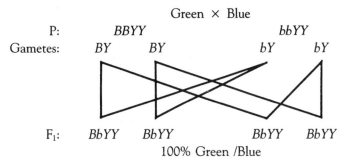

Green × Blue

P: $BBYY$ $bbYY$

Gametes: BY BY bY bY

F_1: $BbYY$ $BbYY$ $BbYY$ $BbYY$

100% Green /Blue

From the cross Green × Blue, birds that have one gene for yellow, one for a lack of yellow, and two for blue are the result.

In the parental generation (P), each animal had a pair of factors for yellow and for blue or for the lack of yellow and for blue, respectively. One therefore designates them as pure, or homozygous. The daughter generation (first filial generation, or F_1), each have one factor for yellow and one for the lack of yellow, as well as two factors for blue. These offspring are called hybrids. They are mixed, or heterozygous with respect to their colors (they must not be confused with hybrids of different species!). What do these birds look like? They are green and cannot be distinguished from their Green parent.

The majority of gene mutations are recessive and may be hidden, as here: in a Peach-faced Lovebird, a factor for the lack of yellow will not be apparent if the bird also has a factor for yellow, which is dominant and hides it. We must therefore differentiate between the external appearance of the bird (phenotype) and its genetic makeup (genotype). In the genotype, the offspring have, of course, one factor for the lack of yellow (*b*) as well as one factor for yellow, so that the characteristic yellow cortex will be evident in the phenotype. (Recessive factors are always symbolized by lower-case letters, as we have done in our inheritance diagrams.)

This result accords completely with the findings which Johann Gregor Mendel revealed as early as 1865 in his work on hybrids in plants (*Versuche mit Pflanzenhybriden*). Mendel experimented primarily with different kinds of peas. The first principle which he put forward reads: If one crosses two pure individuals of a species that differ with respect to a single character, then all hybrids that result are identical. This is the principle of uniformity, or reciprocity, since the same result occurs when one switches the sex of the parents in the cross (reciprocal cross). In our case, therefore, it makes no difference whether the 1,0 or the 0,1 is Blue.

Among breeders, a bird of this F_1 generation is designated as Green /Blue (said "Green split for Blue"). The phenotype is given before a slash, and factors which are hidden in the bird follow a slash.

Strictly speaking, the designation Green /Blue as we have attempted to present it is not correct. Green /lack-of-yellow would be better. But the former expression has probably already become so entrenched that it can no longer be eradicated.

How can one now obtain Blue Peach-faced Lovebirds from the heterozygotes of the F_1 generation? There are two possibilities. With his hybrid peas, Mendel crossed two individuals of the F_1 generation with each other. We can, of course, also do this with Peach-faced Lovebirds.

Green × Blue

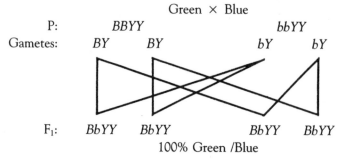

P:	*BBYY*			*bbYY*	
Gametes:	*BY*	*BY*		*bY*	*bY*
F_1:	*BbYY*	*BbYY*		*BbYY*	*BbYY*

100% Green /Blue

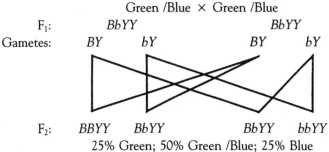

Green /Blue × Green /Blue

F₁: *BbYY*   *BbYY*

Gametes: *BY*   *bY*   *BY*   *bY*

F₂: *BBYY*   *BbYY*   *BbYY*   *bbYY*

25% Green; 50% Green /Blue; 25% Blue

The animals of the F₁ generation can produce gametes that contain either the factors *Y* and *B* or the factors *Y* and *b*. These gametes occur in a 1:1 ratio. At fertilization four combinations of the factors are possible: 25% of the offspring exhibit the factors *BBYY*, 50% the factors *BbYY*, and 25% the factors *bbYY*. Thus, in the genotype we obtain three different variants in the ratio 1:2:1. Phenotypically, on the other hand, we obtain 75% Green and 25% Blue birds, since the heterozygous Peach-faced Lovebirds with the genotype *BbYY* cannot be distinguished from those with the genotype *BBYY*; all are green. For the breeder, this pairing is advisable only in exceptional cases, since he cannot say with certainty whether the green birds are heterozygous for Blue. He can only reckon with the probability that two-thirds of the phenotypically Green birds from this pairing could be split for Blue.

This result of this cross also agrees with the findings of Mendel, who in his second principle states that if one crosses these hybrids (F₁) among themselves, then in the second filial generation (F₂) the traits of dominant-recessive inheritance segregate in the proportions 3:1 (genotype 1:2:1) again. This is called the principle of segregation.

A better pairing in order to again obtain Blue Peach-faced Lovebirds is the so-called backcross. For this purpose one mates a heterozygous animal of the F₁ generation with a homozygous Blue Peach-faced Lovebird.

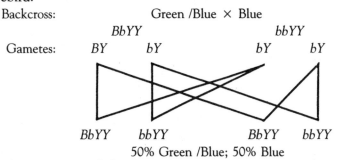

Backcross: Green /Blue × Blue

BbYY   *bbYY*

Gametes: *BY*   *bY*   *bY*   *bY*

BbYY   *bbYY*   *BbYY*   *bbYY*

50% Green /Blue; 50% Blue

A heterozygote of the F₁ generation may just as easily produce gametes that contain the factors *Y* and *B* as those that have *Y* and *b*. But the homozygous bird can only pass on Y and b. Thus, the offspring are 50% Green animals, which are guaranteed to be split for Blue (absence of yellow), and 50% pure Blue animals. This backcross can, of course, also serve as a testcross with the green animals of the F_2 generation. If one pairs such an animal with a Blue bird and all of the offspring are green, then the Peach-faced Lovebird from the F_2 generation was a homozygous Green animal. All of the offspring, of course, are split for Blue. But if just one Blue bird is obtained from this mating, then the green parent from the F_2 generation must have been split for Blue. All siblings of the Blue youngster are therefore certainly split for Blue. One should keep in mind here that a sufficiently large number of offspring must be bred from the pair, since not every brood will correspond to the theoretical ratio. If, however, none of ten young are Blue, one can be almost certain that the green parent is not split for Blue.

For the sake of completeness, it should be added that from a pairing of Blue × Blue, only Blue Peach-faced Lovebirds can result.

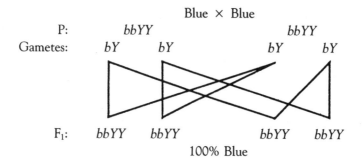

It is also worth noting that one can very easily distinguish the Blue young from the Green ones immediately after hatching. Unlike the Green Peach-faced Lovebirds, which exhibit a rose-colored coat of down, the Blue ones have almost white down.

Since, as was mentioned at the beginning of this chapter, the first Blue came from two Green Peach-faced Lovebirds, then both parents must have been split for Blue. Was this pure chance? Here it should be noted again that factors (genes) which occupy the same position on the two homologous chromosomes affect the same characteristic, namely, cortex color, whether they produce the traits yellow or white. One calls such genes alleles. Homologous genes mutate independently of one another, and so the bird in question will be heterozygous (hybrid) with respect to those particular hereditary factors.

Mutations of this kind certainly occur in nature, but one cannot detect this in an animal. Only when such a bird mates with another that possesses the same mutated, recessive factor does a Blue Peach-faced Lovebird result. The likelihood of this is of course very small, and the event probably occurs only when nestmates pair with one another. If a blue bird should in fact occur in nature, this differently colored animal has a much smaller chance of survival, since it lacks the camouflaging color; a raptor could fix on it better in a flock and hunt it. If the Blue bird happens to survive to sexual maturity and mates with a normal-colored bird, then phenotypically Green birds, which are all split for Blue, will again be the result. Thus, the differently colored animals quickly disappear again.

In captivity, however, such mutations can become apparent if one inbreeds—that is, if one mates related birds with each other. Then the probability is relatively high that at some point two of these recessive factors will occur in the genotype and therefore also be visible in the phenotype.

We can assume with considerable confidence that the first Blue Peach-faced Lovebirds originated from animals related to each other, both of which possessed the recessive factors.

For many years there have been lively discussions among lovebird breeders as to what this variety should really be called. In Germany the name Blue has achieved wide currency. Nevertheless, we wish to advocate the name Pastel-blue, for two reasons: (1) At this time there are no truly blue varieties in Peach-faced Lovebirds; if a really blue variety should happen to occur (and that is not impossible), then the name Blue can be used for it. (2) This color variety is called Pastel-blue internationally as well.

At least one question remains to be solved. Why are the Blue Peach-faced Lovebirds not really blue, but pastel or mignonette blue instead? We wish to attempt to answer this in the section after the next.

Pied Green Peach-faced Lovebirds. In the mid-1960s in the United States (California), a new variety, the Pied, occurred. Jim Hayward (1979) claims that it had already appeared around 1930, but we consider this to be erroneous.

The plumage of birds of this variety is pied with yellow. This piebaldness can be quite variable. One can now find almost totally clear animals that must, however, be genetically designated as pied. The rump and mask remain as they are in the wild-colored animal, although the variegation occasionally extends into the mask. The green areas of the plumage can also be lightened (Light-green), and the flight feathers can be partially white. A few of the claws, sometimes all, are light. Young Pieds can be recognized in the nest because they have a very light bill instead of black at the base of the bill (in a few cases we could detect a little black coloring in minimally pied young).

If we wish to examine the inheritance of Pied more closely, we must first state that all experimental crosses have shown that this mutation exhibits dominant inheritance. This means that a factor for Pied always hides the factor for nonPied (a possible exception will be discussed in detail below). The wild-colored bird has no factor for Pied, but instead possesses factors for nonPied. One must keep this firmly in mind in constructing an inheritance diagram. We wish to introduce the symbol P (dominant) for the factor for Pied and p (recessive) for the nonPied factor. Therefore a Green Peach-faced Lovebird has the following genotype: *BBYYpp*; but a pure Pied Green is *BBYYPP*.

The Pied factor has the effect of preventing the deposition of melanin in some parts of the plumage. Therefore, in these places the blue structural color is eliminated, and the feather is then yellow. The flights, which are almost black in wild birds and therefore contain no yellow, must, of course, appear white with the absence of melanin.

If we pair a pure Pied with a pure Green Peach-faced Lovebird, then the inheritance diagram looks like this:

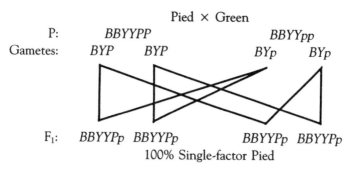

Pied × Green

P:	*BBYYPP*	*BBYYpp*
Gametes:	*BYP* *BYP*	*BYp* *BYp*

F_1: *BBYYPp* *BBYYPp*   *BBYYPp* *BBYYPp*

100% Single-factor Pied

Since the Pied bird can only produce gametes containing the factors *BYP*, and the wild-colored bird only those with the factors *BYp*, then all of the young will receive one factor for Pied and one for nonPied.

Therefore, they are all piebald, since this factor is of course dominant, and the factor for nonPied is not visible. The young cannot be distinguished from the Pied parent.

If one now crosses the young from the F_1 generation with Green Peach-faced Lovebirds, then we get the result shown in the diagram below:

Backcross: Single-factor Pied (F_1) × Green
                  BBYYPp   *BBYYpp*

Gametes: *BYP*   *BYp*   *BYp*   *BYp*

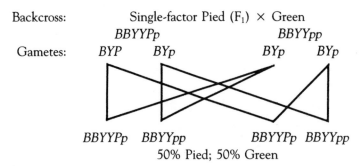

BBYYPp   BBYYpp   BBYYPp   BBYYpp
50% Pied; 50% Green

The Pieds of the F_1 generation can produce gametes which have either the factors *BYP* or *BYp*, whereas the Green bird can only produce gametes with the factors *BYp*. Thus half of the progeny are Pied and half are Green.

Here too there are several other pairing possibilities, for which we only wish to set down the expectations, since the breeder can quickly draw the inheritance diagram himself. In the following, *PP* = Pied with two factors for Pied; *Pp* = Pied with one factor for Pied and one for nonPied; *pp* = Green Peach-faced with two factors for nonPied.

- Pied (*PP*) × Pied (*PP*) = 100% Pied (*PP*)
- Pied (*PP*) × Pied (*Pp*) = 50% Pied (*PP*); 50% Pied (*Pp*)
- Pied (*PP*) × Green (*pp*) = 100% Pied (*Pp*)
- Pied (*Pp*) × Pied (*Pp*) = 50% Pied (*Pp*); 25% Pied (*PP*); 25% Green (*pp*)
- Pied (*Pp*) × Green (*pp*) = 50% Pied (*Pp*); 50% Green (*pp*)

At this point we should again point out that the Pied factor is inherited dominantly. This means that, as the breeder says, no animals can be split for Pied. Unfortunately, there are still breeders who sell animals as such splits to unsuspecting fanciers; or do these breeders themselves not know any better?

We have already indicated that the piebaldness can be extremely variable. The first Pieds in California are said to have had only a yellow patch on the head. In the course of time, increasingly clearer Pieds have been bred through selection, so that birds now exist that are almost completely yellow, and which are also often sold as Yellows. Nevertheless, these birds are Pieds and, of course, also pass on the Pied factor dominantly. One cannot, however, predict the extent of piebaldness in the plumage. In our broods, for example, from animals slightly pied with yellow, almost clear Pieds frequently appear, and vice versa. Most breeders prefer this course: heavily pied paired with one that shows little variegation.

Today, heavily pied birds are greatly admired by fanciers. For exhibition purposes, however, Pieds must have pied markings that are clearly defined, not washed out, and as symmetrical as possible. They should exhibit an ideal color distribution of 50%:50% (as in the AZ-DKB standard). As soon as Blue and Pied Green Peach-faced Lovebirds were both available, many breeders naturally attempted to combine these two varieties into a new color combination.

Pied Blue Peach-faced Lovebirds. A combination of the Blue and the Pied factors is actually not very difficult, provided one has become somewhat familiar with the principles of inheritance. We can begin with a Blue bird and a Pied Green one. Let us recall that the Blue Peach-faced Lovebird has two factors for a lack of yellow and two factors for structural blue. In addition, it must also possess two factors for nonPied; i.e., *bbYYpp*. The pure Pied Green has two factors for yellow, two for blue, and two for Pied *BBYYPP*. Our inheritance diagram looks like this:

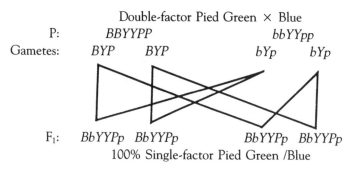

Double-factor Pied Green × Blue

P: *BBYYPP*   *bbYYpp*

Gametes: *BYP*   *BYP*   *bYp*   *bYp*

F₁: *BbYYPp BbYYPp*   *BbYYPp BbYYPp*
100% Single-factor Pied Green /Blue

The Pied can only pass on the factors *B*, *Y*, and *P*; the Blue bird only the factors *b*, *Y*, and *p*. All direct offspring of these two birds (F₁) therefore have the genotype *BbYYPp*. *B* is dominant over *b*, so the birds' feathers have a yellow cortex. The blue structural color is produced by the factor *Y*. The ground color of this Peach-faced Lovebird is therefore green. *P* is dominant over *p*, so the Pied factor is of course

Lutino Peach-faced Lovebird.

apparent in the phenotype. The birds of the F_1 generation are thus Pied Greens, but they carry a factor for absence of yellow (*b*) and are therefore split for Blue. To be completely accurate, we must in fact say that they are split not only for Blue, but also for nonPied, since they do after all have the factor *p* in the genotype. The breeder calls them single-factor Pieds.

The next step would be a backcross pairing a bird from the F_1 generation (Pied Green /Blue) with a Blue bird.

Backcross: Blue × Pied Green /Blue

bbYYpp	*BbYYPp*			
⇩	*BYP*	*BYp*	*bYP*	*bYp*
bYp	*BbYYPp*	*BbYYpp*	*bbYYPp*	*bbYYpp*
bYp	*BbYYPp*	*BbYYpp*	*bbYYPp*	*bbYYpp*

25% each: Single-factor Pied Green /Blue;
Green /Blue; Single-factor Pied Blue; Blue

The Pied Green /Blue from the F_1 generation can produce gametes which contain the factors *BYP, BYp, bYP,* or *bYP*. Thus there are—we wish to point this out one more time—four different combinations possible for the factors in this animal's gametes. This is only true, of course, when the alleles are on three different chromosomes. This condition does happen to be satisfied here, as all experimental crosses have demonstrated.

The Blue bird can only produce gametes that contain the factors *bYp*. For this reason we have considered only one of the Blue Peach-faced Lovebird's gametes in the inheritance diagram.

Thus, from this mating we obtain young with the genotypes *BbYYPp, BbYYpp, bbYYPp,* and *bbYYpp* in the ratio 1:1:1:1, or 25% each. Now, what do these birds look like, what is their phenotype?

We are already familiar with Peach-faced Lovebirds of the genotype *BbYYPp*. They have one factor for the yellow cortex (dominant), the factors for the blue structural color, and one factor for Pied, and are therefore single-factor Pied Green /Blue.

We also already know the birds with the genotype *ByYYpp*. They again have a yellow cortex, the blue structural color, but no Pied factor (i.e., two factors for nonPied), and are therefore Green /Blue.

The genotype *bbYYPp* has not yet been encountered, but we can easily determine its phenotype. Two factors for lack of yellow in the cortex, two factors for blue structural color, and one factor for Pied (dominant), so here a single-factor Pied Blue must have been produced.

The fourth possibility (*bbYYpp*) can be quickly identified: no yellow in the cortex, blue structural color present, no factor for Pied; so these must be Blue Peach-faced Lovebirds.

In summary this means that, if we pair a single-factor Yellow-pied Green /Blue with a Blue Peach-faced Lovebird, then we obtain young in the colors Green /Blue, single-factor Pied Green /Blue, single-factor Pied Blue, and Blue—25% of each.

This is in agreement with Mendel's third principle, which states that the genetic factors are inherited independently of one another, forming new combinations during the formation of the gametes (principle of independence of genetic factors, or the recombination of the genes). However, the principle applies only when the factors lie on different chromosomes, as we already mentioned above. The chromosomes were unknown to Mendel, remember.

It should be noticed that the Pied Blues we have been considering are pied with yellow. Shouldn't Blues pied with white actually have occurred, since we have, after all, stated that the blue structural color is in places eliminated from the plumage by the Pied factor. The Blue bird, so we said, has no yellow in its plumage. If the blue is also eliminated from the feathers that do not show any yellow, then these would have to look white! Pieds in Blue appear to be yellow-pied Blue, however, though the yellow is not rich as in the Pied Greens, but instead is a light, creamy yellow. Often the blue is also much lighter in these Pieds.

It must here be remembered that in the description of the Blue Peach-faced Lovebird we called attention to the fact that it is not a matter of a clear, rich blue, but instead of a pastel or mignonette color. How can this be explained?

Since we do not find any white feathers in Pied Blue Peach-faced Lovebirds, contrary to what can be assumed theoretically, two possibilities present themselves. It is conceivable that the gene that affects the yellow color in the cortex of the feathers has not mutated in such a way that completely prevents the deposition of yellow pigments in the feathers; instead, psittacin, if greatly reduced, is still vestigially present. This would explain the pastel blue coloration of the Blue Peach-faced Lovebird, as well as the light yellow feathers in the Pied Blue. If this indeed is the case, then at this time we cannot produce a genuine blue

Facing page: Wild-colored (Green) Peach-faced Lovebird.

Experiments have shown that distinct genes, each of which plays some role in melanin deposition, are responsible for the Edged-yellow (left) and Lutino (below) Peach-faced Lovebird varieties.

Peach-faced Lovebird and, of course, no white-pied Blue either. So we must wait for a further mutation of this factor.

Another possibility would be that a second factor is responsible for the light yellow color of the cortex. This possibility is also accepted by some breeders (see Ochs 1980). Nevertheless, it seems to us very questionable to designate this factor as simply the "Yellow-face factor" (in imitation of Budgerigar genetics). We feel it is completely erroneous to assume that this Yellow-face factor, a dominant factor from the Pied Green, has been carried over to the Pied Blue, as is stated in the AZ-DKB standard. If this were the case, then this Yellow-face factor could have been eliminated very quickly through selective breeding, since the nonPieds should not exhibit this factor. If such a second factor does exist, it must also occur in wild-colored and Blue birds and in all other color varieties (see, for example, Albino). In this case also, we must wait for this factor to mutate to obtain genuine blue or White-pied Blue *roseicollis*. We will consider this problem again in the section on prospects for the future.

We cannot say with certainty which of these two assumptions is actually correct, since this problem has by no means been solved. We suspect, however, that it does involve some second factor that attenuates the deposition of the yellow pigment, throughout the entire plumage, of course, and in all known color varieties.

In our opinion, Ochs is quite correct when he writes that today with Peach-faced Lovebirds it is no longer really a problem to maintain new varieties or color combinations and to propagate them; instead, the big problems involve correct designations for the color varieties. If, in our explanations, we too write about "Blue" or "Pied Blue" Peach-faced Lovebirds for short, we do so with the understanding that it would be better to call them "Pastel-blue" or "Pied Pastel-blue."

Let us now, however, return to the inheritance of the Pied factor in the Blue birds. The reader surely understands that within the constraints of this book not all pairing possibilities can be diagrammed. With a little practice, however, any fancier can do this for his breeding pairs himself. Two further examples should clarify the inheritance:

From the pairing of double-factor Pied Green $\times$ Blue we obtained single-factor Pied Green /Blue in the F_1. These birds had the genotype *BbYYPp*. How does the inheritance work if we pair two such F_1 birds with each other?

Single-factor Pied Green /Blue × Single-factor Pied Green /Blue
BbYYPp   *BbYYPp*

♀ \ ♂	*BYP*	*BYp*	*bYP*	*bYp*
BYP	*BBYYPP*	*BBYYPp*	*BbYYPP*	*BbYYPp*
BYp	*BBYYPp*	*BBYYpp*	*BbYYPp*	*BbYYpp*
bYP	*BbYYPP*	*BbYYPp*	*bbYYPP*	*bbYYPp*
bYp	*BbYYPp*	*BbYYpp*	*bbYYPp*	*bbYYpp*

Since both birds can produce gametes that have either the factors *BYP, BYp, bYP,* or *bYP,* sixteen possible combinations of these gametes can occur at fertilization. In the F_2 generation the following young can hatch: $\frac{1}{16}$ = 6.25% Double-factor Pied Green (*BBYYPP*); $\frac{2}{16}$ = 12.50% Single-factor Pied Green (*BBYYPp*); $\frac{2}{16}$ = 12.50% Double-factor Pied Green /Blue (*BbYYPP*); $\frac{4}{16}$ = 25.00% Single-factor Pied Green /Blue (*BbYYPp*); $\frac{1}{16}$ = 6.25% Green (*BBYYpp*); $\frac{2}{16}$ = 12.50% Green /Blue (*BbYYpp*); $\frac{1}{16}$ = 6.25% Double-factor Pied Blue (*bbYYPP*); $\frac{2}{16}$ = 12.50% Single-factor Pied Blue (*bbYYPp*); $\frac{1}{16}$ = 6.25% Blue (*bbYYpp*).

Thus, we obtain four different varieties (phenotypes), though in quite different proportions. The breeder must clearly understand, however, that he would not be able to distinguish, for example, the very different genotypes of the Pied Greens, which are all identical phenotypically. This, of course, also holds true for the Pied Blues and the Green birds. The genotypes of the F_2 generation can be ascertained through planned backcrosses (testcrosses). For serious color breeding, this pairing would therefore be unsuitable. Of more interest, certainly, would be a cross between Peach-faced Lovebirds which are single-factor Pied Green /Blue (*BbYYPp*) and single-factor Pied Blue (*bbYYPp*).

Single-factor Pied Blue × Single-factor Pied Green /Blue
bbYYPp   *BbYYPp*

♀ \ ♂	*BYP*	*BYp*	*bYP*	*bYp*
bYP	*BbYYPP*	*BbYYPp*	*bbYYPP*	*bbYYPp*
bYp	*BbYYPp*	*BbYYpp*	*bbYYPp*	*bbYYpp*

The following young can result: $\frac{1}{8}$ = 12.5% Double-factor Pied Green /Blue (*BbYYPP*); $\frac{2}{8}$ = 25.0% Single-factor Pied Green /Blue

The Edged-white Peach-faced Lovebird is produced by combining the Blue and the Edged-yellow factors.

Facing page: As the primary feathers of the Green Peach-faced Lovebird exhibit extensive melanin coloration, they are much altered by those mutations that affect the melanins.

A further combination of color factors is found in the Peach-faced variety known as Pied Edged-white.

(*BbYYPp*); ⅛ = 12.5% Double-factor Pied Blue (*bbYYPP*); ²⁄₈ = 25.0% Single-factor Pied Blue (*bbYYPp*); ⅛ = 12.5% Green /Blue (*BbYYpp*); ⅛ = 12.5% Blue (*bbYYpp*).

This pairing has the great advantage that one can guarantee that all of the young which are Pied Green or Green are also split for Blue. Whether the Pieds have only one factor for Pied or two can be ascertained through another controlled pairing.

In the pairing of Blue birds and Pied Blues, or of Pied Blues among themselves, the results are the same as those presented in the section on Pied Greens.

Young Pied Blues can easily be recognized in the nest as well, since they have almost white-brown plumage and a light bill, like the Blues.

The Pied Blues with red bills occasionally offered are young birds, which have a carrot-colored bill. This color is lost after the first molt.

We have already pointed out that heavily pied animals can occur in the Pied Blues as well. In some cases, these Pieds can even lose the reddish frontal band; they then truly look creamy and are sometimes offered under the name "Creams." These are indeed Pieds, however, which of course also transmit their genes as such. These animals are not valuable for exhibition, because the previously mentioned AZ-DKB standard stipulates that the birds exhibit pied markings as clearly defined as possible and ideal color proportions of 50%:50%. The hobbyist breeder, on the other hand, prefers very clear Pieds.

Recessive-pied Peach-faced Lovebirds. It should certainly be clear to any reader of the two previous sections that no Peach-faced Lovebirds can be split for Pied, since the factor for Pied is dominant. We have, however, very frequently heard from breeder friends in Holland that Recessive-pieds may have existed there or still do. This means that a second mutation, in which Pied is inherited through recessive factors, may exist. This mutation has nothing to do with the dominantly inherited Pied, of course. Also, it becomes visible only when a bird has two factors for Recessive-pied. At this time we cannot confirm that such birds exist nor can we deny it.

We (Brockmann) subsequently obtained a pair of Green Peach-faced Lovebirds from a breeder friend, Herr Enting of Emsdetten. In one brood for him, besides two Greens, they also reared a yellow-pied green youngster. The two parents were absolutely green, not even one claw was light. In a second brood (for us), this pair produced four Green young. Unfortunately, the hen died of an ovarian inflammation, so that further breeding with this pair was impossible. But since we also had the Pied Green youngster in our possession, we undertook controlled pairings. All matings between the green offspring, even those with the father, brought only green young. No breeding was successful with the Pied, because he died in an accident. The existence of Recessive-pieds therefore could not be proved. In the event that similar cases are known somewhere, we would be very grateful if someone would inform us about them. Perhaps in the future we can one day say with certainty whether recessively inherited Pieds exist (see Australian-pied below).

Perhaps almost completely clear Pieds also result from the combination of dominant and recessive Pieds, as is known in Budgerigar breeding (Black-eyed Clears).

Yellow Peach-faced Lovebirds. This variety, also called Japanese Golden Cherry among us, has almost pure yellow plumage which, however, is tinged with a very light green. The flights are whitish light gray, the mask red, the rump light blue, and the eyes black. These birds first occurred in 1954 for Masaru Iwata of Japan. The color of the parents is not known to us.

How this yellow variety comes about is easily explained. The structure of a feather should again be recalled; simplified, it looks like this:

Through a new mutation, the factor for the blue structural color has changed; it is now eliminated. More precisely, melanin is no longer deposited in the medulla, so the dark background is lacking and all the light is reflected. But since the cortex remains yellow in the Yellow Peach-faced Lovebird, the bird is also yellow.

Our simplified feather cross-section therefore looks like this:

yellow
+   = yellow bird
absence of blue

If we again wish to represent the genotype with symbols, then *B* stands for the presence of yellow and *y* for a lack of blue, since the factor for a lack of blue is recessive to the factor for blue (*Y,* or nonYel-

Pied Edged-yellow Peach-faced Lovebird. The pied areas show no evidence of the vestigial melanin that characterizes the Edged-yellow.

Facing page: Lutino and Green Peach-faced Lovebirds.

A combination of the Blue and the Yellow factors is responsible for the White Peach-faced Lovebird.

low). Thus the Yellow Peach-faced Lovebird has the genotype *BByy*.

If we cross a Yellow animal with a Green bird, then the inheritance is as follows:

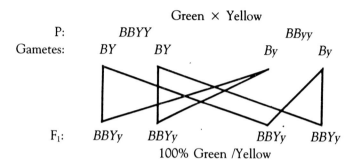

All offspring of these two homozygous animals would then have the factors *BBYy*. The factor *B* produces the yellow cortex. The factor *Y* stands for the blue-structural-color trait, since *Y* is dominant over *y* (absence of blue). So all of the birds of the F₁ generation are Green but split for Yellow, as a breeder would say.

If one crosses these birds of the F₁ generation among themselves, this results:

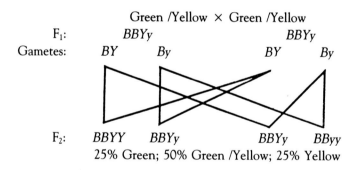

The F₂-generation offspring with the genotype *BBYY* are of course Green birds, and those with *BBYy* are also Green Peach-faced Lovebirds, but they are split for Yellow. Only the animals with the genotype *BByy* are Yellow. With the Green birds we cannot tell which are split for Yellow, since they are all identical phenotypically. Only controlled pairings (backcrossing) can give us information about these animals' genotypes. The results of the first and the second crosses again accord with Mendel's principles.

A backcross would look like this:

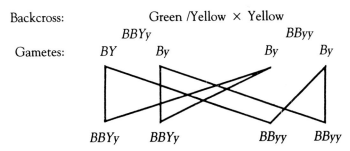

Backcross: Green /Yellow × Yellow

Of the offspring, half are Green /Yellow and half are Yellow. If one crosses two Yellow Peach-faced Lovebirds with each other, then all the offspring must of course also be Yellow, since the parents are pure for the trait.

If Blue as well as Yellow Peach-faced Lovebirds are available, it is actually very easy to consider a combination of these two varieties as well.

White Peach-faced Lovebirds. Before we discuss the White Peach-faced Lovebird (also called Japanese Silver Cherry) in greater detail, we wish first to explain how it occurs.

If a mutation in which the cortex is no longer yellow (the Blue Peach-faced Lovebird) is available, and when there exists another mutation in which the blue structural color is lacking (the Yellow Peach-faced Lovebird), then experienced breeders naturally strive to combine both mutations in one bird.

Let us recall once more that the Blue bird has the factors $bbYY$ (b = factor for the lack of psittacin, Y = factor for structural blue), and the Yellow one possesses $BByy$ (B = factor for yellow, y = factor for the absence of blue). Pairing these two birds takes the following course:

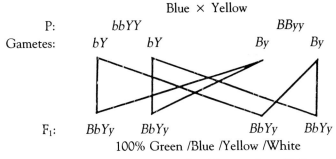

All offspring from the mating of a Blue with a Yellow Peach-faced Lovebird have the genotype $BbYy$, since the Blue bird can pass on only

111

The Lutino Peach-faced Lovebird exhibits a complete absence of melanin pigmentation.

Facing page: In this Edged-White Peach-faced Lovebird, the effect of the Edged-yellow factor is obvious to the eye.

The Albino Peach-faced Lovebird, in which the Blue factor is combined with the Ino.

bY and the Yellow only *yB*. The factor for yellow in the feather cortex is dominant over the one for the lack of yellow, just as the factor for blue is dominant over the factor for the lack of blue; therefore, all birds of the F_1 generation are Green! But all of these Peach-faced Lovebirds do in fact have the factors *b* and *y*, so they are split not only for Yellow and for Blue, and also for White, as we wish to demonstrate.

If one now crosses birds of the F_1 generation with each other, the following inheritance diagram results:

Green /Yellow /Blue /White × Green /Yellow /Blue /White
BbYy   *BbYy*

	BY	*By*	*bY*	*by*
BY	*BBYY*	*BBYy*	*BbYY*	*BbYy*
By	*BBYy*	*BByy*	*BbYy*	*Bbyy*
bY	*BbYY*	*BbYy*	*bbYY*	*bbYy*
by	*BbYy*	*Bbyy*	*bbYy*	*bbyy*

Since the birds of the F_1 generation can form gametes that contain either the factors *BY, By, bY,* or *by*, then sixteen possibilities at fertilization again result. These sixteen possibilities can very easily be read from the genotypes in the following; the phenotypes are also easy to interpret, if we remember the meanings of the symbols: $\frac{1}{16}$ = 6.25% Green (*BBYY*); $\frac{2}{16}$ = 12.50% Green /Yellow (*BBYy*); $\frac{2}{16}$ = 12.50% Green /Blue (*BbYY*); $\frac{4}{16}$ = 25.00% Green /Blue /Yellow /White (*BbYy*); $\frac{1}{16}$ = 6.25% Yellow (*BByy*); $\frac{2}{16}$ = 12.50% Yellow /White (*Bbyy*); $\frac{1}{16}$ = 6.25% Blue (*bbYY*); $\frac{2}{16}$ = 12.50% Blue /White (*bbYy*); $\frac{1}{16}$ = 6.25% White (*bbyy*).

Thus, the White bird is one of the results of the F_1-generation cross. The 6.25% means, of course, that only a small portion of the young in the F_2 generation are White, namely about six out of one hundred. But this was certainly the way in which these birds were produced initially.

In the White Peach-faced Lovebird, the two mutations have been brought together; that is, this bird lacks yellow in the cortex of its feathers and no longer shows the blue structural color. Therefore, the simplified cross-section of a feather must look like this:

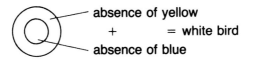

Unfortunately, this bird does not look white, however. For now, this is still wishful thinking on the part of all breeders. The explanation lies in the fact that the color of this Peach-faced Lovebird is a combination of the colors of the Pastel-blue and the Yellow birds. Unfortunately, as we have previously written in our discussion of the Pied Pastel-blue, the Pastel-blue animal does not exhibit a truly blue color. Also, a vestige of yellow is also retained by our White Peach-faced Lovebird, so that it has very light yellow plumage with a light green tinge. An accurate designation for this color is, unfortunately, not yet in general use, so that it will certainly continue to be offered by breeders under the name Japanese Silver Cherry.

Yellow and White Peach-faced Lovebirds are certainly very attractive birds, since they have already won top awards at many exhibitions. They are also correspondingly more expensive to purchase. At this point, however, we wish to draw attention to a problem in the breeding of these varieties, which is certainly no longer a mystery to the fancier who is seriously occupied with them. Although we contacted a great number of breeders to collect as much material as possible for this work, we encountered virtually no breeders of these varieties who had ever reared any offspring from a Yellow or a White Peach-faced Lovebird female. To state it even more explicitly, the Yellow and White (Japanese-origin) females lay eggs from which—as far as we know—almost no young hatch. In some cases, the egg white is as thin as water or is interspersed with many small air bubbles; occasionally even the yolk is lacking. We have ascertained that an embryo very rarely develops in these eggs, and it almost always dies after a short time. We cannot determine at this time whether this is caused by a lethal (fatal) factor. Such lethal factors are best known to bird breeders from crested Budgerigars and crested Canaries. In one case, it was reported to us that a Belgian breeder bred a Green youngster from a Yellow hen; however, we were not able to verify this.

Christ (1983) reported that in his breeding facility a Peach-faced Lovebird pair, 1,0 Pied Green /Edged-yellow × 0,1 Yellow, had five eggs, from which two young hatched; of these, one died.

Thus, these varieties apparently offer the fancier only the following crossing possibilities: (1) 1,0 Yellow × 0,1 Green /Yellow = 50% Yel-

The presence of a single Dark factor in a Peach-faced Lovebird produces the variety called Dark-green.

Facing page: Pied Olive Peach-faced Lovebird. The unpied areas of the plumage evince the effect of the Dark factor.

The shade of green in the Olive Peach-faced Lovebird is the result of the doubled Dark factor.

low and 50% Green /Yellow; (2) 1,0 Green /Yellow × 0,1 Green /Yellow = 25% Green, 50% Green /Yellow, and 25% Yellow. One can, of course, also pair 1,0 Blue /White, White, Yellow /White, or Green /Blue /Yellow /White, with 0,1 Blue /White or Green /Blue /Yellow /White. The results of these crosses can be obtained from the list of expectations for the varieties of *Agapornis personata*. It should also be noted that Yellow Peach-faced Lovebirds that are also split for White have almost no green tinge to their plumage.

Pied Yellow and Pied White Peach-faced Lovebirds. Some breeders are now attempting to cross Pied factors into Yellow and White Peach-faced Lovebirds. They hope that then the female animals will perhaps be fertile. So far, we only know that such a female had had fertile eggs several times, but no young hatched (Ochs, *in litt.*).

Yet we can breed Pied Yellows. They already exist. The birds hardly show the Pied factor at all, which of course is easily explained. With extensive distribution of piebaldness, the green tinge disappears, and possibly even the red mask. Pied White Peach-faced Lovebirds can also be bred if one crosses Pied into the White Peach-faced Lovebird. It is not known to us whether these animals already exist. We assume, however, that the light green tinge in the plumage is also absent from these birds if the piebaldness is very pronounced.

We wish to illustrate crossing Pied into the Yellow or White Peach-faced Lovebirds by this example:

We mate a 1,0 Yellow (no Pied factors) with a 0,1 double-factor Pied Blue: $BByypp \times bbYYPP$. The diagram will look like this:

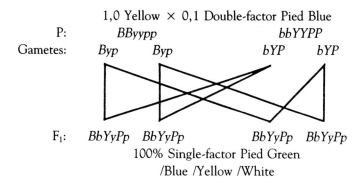

1,0 Yellow × 0,1 Double-factor Pied Blue

P: $BByypp$ $bbYYPP$

Gametes: Byp Byp bYP bYP

F₁: $BbYyPp$ $BbYyPp$ $BbYyPp$ $BbYyPp$
100% Single-factor Pied Green
/Blue /Yellow /White

From this pairing only birds that have the factors $BbYyPp$ can occur. These birds are Pied Greens, since the factors B, Y, and P are dominant

118

to *b, y,* and *p.* All young of the F₁ generation, however, are heterozygous for Blue, Yellow, and White, as well as nonPied.

The Peach-faced Lovebirds of the F_1 generation produce gametes which could contain the following factors: *BYP, BYp, ByP, Byp, bYP, bYp, byP,* and *byp*—eight different combinations. If we mate two young animals from the F_1 generation, sixty-four possibilities in the union of the gametes of these animals would result. Such a diagram would, however, exceed the constraints of this book, so we must do without one in this instance. Nevertheless, it should be clear to the reader that this cross will result in some animals with the genotype *bbyyPp* or *bbyyPP,* that is, the Pied Whites.

There are certainly many other ways to obtain animals of this kind. For example, one can cross the F_1 young with Blue, Yellow or even White animals. The last course would certainly be the easiest. The expectations look like this:

- 1,0 White (*bbyypp*) × 0,1 Single-factor Yellow-pied Green /Blue /Yellow /White (*BbYyPp*) = 12.50% Single-factor Yellow-pied Green /Blue /Yellow /White (*BbYyPp*); 12.50% Green /Blue /Yellow /White (*BbYypp*); 12.50% Single-factor Pied Yellow /White (*BbyyPp*); 12.50% Yellow /White (*Bbyypp*); 12.50% Yellow-pied Blue /White (*bbYyPp*); 12.50% Blue /White (*bbYypp*); 12.50% Single-factor Yellow-pied White (*bbyyPp*); 12.50% White (*bbyypp*)

This pairing offers the great advantage that one can say with certainty that all of the young are split for White if they are not phenotypically White.

Edged-yellow Peach-faced Lovebirds. This variety is also called American Golden Cherry by many breeders, since it is said to have originated in America.

The feathers of this variety are a greenish yellow, and the wing and also the back feathers have a distinct dark edging. For this reason they are called Edged-yellow. The eyes are dark, the rump washed-out blue; the red mask resembles that of the wild bird, and the claws are lighter than in Green animals.

For many years, there was a great deal of confusion about this variety, since one did not know with certainty whether it was a separate mutation or a kind of Yellow Peach-faced Lovebird. We know today that it really is a new variety, and we wish to explain this briefly.

Controlled pairings with Yellow (Japanese-origin) Peach-faced Lovebirds provided a clear picture: all offspring were Green! Some readers

Pied Olive Peach-faced Lovebird, a combination of the Pied and the Dark factors.

Facing page: As further combinations of color varieties are undertaken, it becomes less easy to assess genotypes. Designating these Peach-faced Lovebirds as Dark-greens doesn't seem to explain their appearance sufficiently.

Pied Green Peach-faced Lovebird, a youngster.

will certainly now ask whether this result is truly unequivocal. Fundamentally it is very simple. If one crosses an Edged-yellow Peach-faced Lovebird with a Yellow (Japanese origin), and both belonged to the same variety and therefore also possessed the same factors (*BByy*), then the offspring would all have to be Yellow. This was not the case, however. Moreover, one can draw another conclusion from the above-mentioned result. Since the Yellow bird has no factor for the Blue structural color, as all previous inheritance diagrams have shown, but the young from the controlled pairing are Green, then the Edged-yellow bird must still possess the factors of blue, just as they occur in the wild-colored bird: that is, not mutated at all. Only in this way can the green color of the offspring be explained.

We wish to designate the Edged-yellow factor, when we have further occasion to represent it, as *e*. If we introduce this designation, then we must of course not forget that the wild-colored bird has a factor for nonEdged-yellow, which we must also designate in order to set forth our inheritance diagram with appropriate clarity; we wish to represent this factor with *E*.

A normal green Peach-faced Lovebird therefore has the factors *BBYYEE*, and an Edged-yellow has *BBYYee*. If we cross two such animals then we obtain the following result:

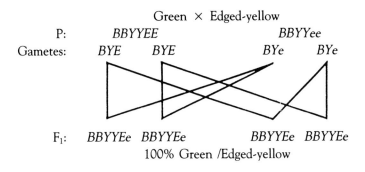

Green × Edged-yellow

P:	*BBYYEE*			*BBYYee*	
Gametes:	*BYE*	*BYE*		*BYe*	*BYe*

F₁: *BBYYEe*   *BBYYEe*   *BBYYEe*   *BBYYEe*
100% Green /Edged-yellow

All direct offspring of this pair will have the genotype *BBYYEe*. The factor *E* for nonEdged-yellow is dominant to the factor *e* (Edged-yellow), so all of the birds are Green, but split for Edged-yellow.

If one again crosses the birds from the F₁ generation with one another, then one obtains:

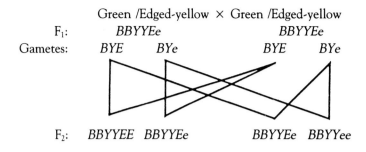

Green /Edged-yellow × Green /Edged-yellow

F₁: BBYYEe   BBYYEe
Gametes: BYE   BYe   BYE   BYe

F₂: BBYYEE BBYYEe   BBYYEe BBYYee

In the F₂ generation we again obtain 25% Green, 50% Green /Edged-yellow, and 25% Edged-yellow, since only the presence of two of the recessive factors (*ee*) produces the edged feathers. Just what in the feather structure is changed by these factors has not yet been explained. We assume, however, that the structural color is diminished, either through altered melanin deposition or changes in the cloudy cells. The factors for the blue structural color are present as before, however.

Further pairing expectations will not be diagrammed; only the results will be given:

- Edged-yellow × Green /Edged-yellow = 50% Green /Edged-yellow; 50% Edged-yellow.
- Green /Edged-yellow × Green /Edged-yellow = 25% Green; 50% Green /Edged-yellow; 25% Edged-yellow.
- Green /Edged-yellow × Green = 50% Green; 50% Green /Edged-yellow.

Edged-white Peach-faced Lovebirds. Edged-white Peach-faced Lovebirds, also called American Silver Cherries, are a result of crosses between Pastel-blue and Edged-yellow birds (see also the section on the White Peach-faced Lovebird). These birds have an ash gray color in their plumage, which is tinged with green, however. The forehead is pink, the cheeks and the throat light gray with a light pink luster. A dark edging on the back and wing feathers is clearly recognizable. One can breed Edged-whites from Edged-yellows in two generations, which is no mystery to the experienced breeder. One mates an Edged-yellow bird with a Blue, which of course has no factor for Edged-yellow.

A Mauve Peach-faced Lovebird, which adds the Blue factor to the doubled Dark factor.

Facing page: Dark-factor Peach-faced Lovebirds.

In the Blue series, a single Dark factor produces the Peach-faced variety called Dark-blue, or Cobalt.

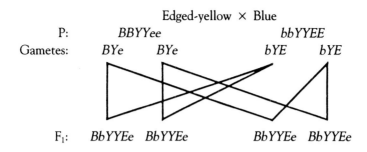

Edged-yellow × Blue

P: *BBYYee*   *bbYYEE*

Gametes: *BYe*   *BYe*   *bYE*   *bYE*

F_1:   *BbYYEe*   *BbYYEe*   *BbYYEe*   *BbYYEe*

In the F_1 generation we obtain only birds that have the factors *BbYYEe*, so they are Green /Blue /Edged-yellow /Edged-white, since they do have the factors *bYe*. The next step would be to pair these young with each other.

At this point, it should be added that in the instances in which we speak of pairing young of the F_1 generation, we do not mean that the breeder should practice inbreeding. Such a course should only be chosen in exceptional cases. It would be better to set up two pairs and then cross the young from these pairs with each other.

If one mates the birds of the F_1 generation (*BbYYEe*) with each other, then animals having the factors *bbYYee* can occur. These are the Edged-white Peach-faced Lovebirds described above. They lack the yellow in the cortex, except for the amount that is still present in the feathers as a result of the factors of the Pastel-blue bird. In addition, the blue structural color is much lighter in them.

Pied Edged-yellow Peach-faced Lovebirds. When the Edged-yellow Peach-faced Lovebirds came to Europe from the United States, there was not only the puzzle about the mutation itself. The confusion was magnified because many varieties of these animals were offered. They arrived as "American Golden Cherry Greens" or "American Golden Cherry Clears." In these birds (Edged-yellow with the Pied factor) the blue structural color is almost totally absent from some feathers—or, if the piebaldness is very pronounced, from almost the entire plumage— thus these birds are in many cases really extremely yellow, but of course they retain their dark eyes. Occasionally, one can even in the nest i- dentify such completely clear Pied Edged-yellow birds (which are much in demand among fanciers), since their eyes glitter dark red through the still closed lids in the early stages of life, though later this appearance is lost.

An inheritance diagram can be omitted, since the reader is certainly now in the position to draw it himself. These instructions should provide a little help: Edged-yellow (*BBYYppee*) × Yellow-pied Green (*BBYYPPEE*) produces in the F$_1$ generation *BBYYPpEe* which is single-factor Pied Green /Edged-yellow. If these are again paired with Edged-yellow, among others, one obtains birds with the genotype *BBYYPpee*, namely, Pied Edged-yellow Peach-faced Lovebirds.

Pied Edged-white Peach-faced Lovebirds. One now thinks of crossing the dominant Pied factor into the Edged-white as well. Such birds have already existed for a number of years. It is, of course, best to choose Pied Blues for the cross, since they no longer possess the factor for yellow cortex (*B*)—for example, *bbYYPPEE*. If one crosses such a bird with an Edged-white (*bbYYppee*) in the F$_1$ generation, one obtains birds with the genotype *bbYYPpEe*. If these are again backcrossed with Edged-white Peach-faced Lovebirds having the factors *bbYYPpee*, then Pied Edged-white Peach-faced Lovebirds, are obtained, among others. In these birds, as in the Pieds with Edged-yellow, the color will be lightened, depending upon how pronounced the piebaldness is.

It is, of course, also possible to pair Edged-yellow or Edged-white Peach-faced Lovebirds with Yellow or White (Japanese origin) birds, producing birds that possess the traits of both. To the best of our knowledge, this has not yet been done, so we cannot say how these birds look. In addition, one could also cross the factor for Pied into these animals, so that one could obtain the following color combinations: Yellow Edged-yellow Peach-faced Lovebirds, and these in Pied; and White Edged-white Peach-faced Lovebirds, and these in Pied as well. Whether these color combinations are a worthwhile breeding goal will not be considered. Certainly the danger exists that one might be unable to classify these birds phenotypically.

Fallow Peach-faced Lovebirds. Fallow Peach-faced Lovebirds are a distinct new mutation that occurred in 1977 in East Germany (Lehmann and Seidel 1980) and probably also about the same time in West Germany (Grau, oral comm.). As yet very few of them exist. In the Netherlands and in Belgium Fallows or splits can be found occasionally. What follows describes the Fallows that have occurred in West Germany.

As youngsters, these birds have dirty yellowish green plumage, but can be recognized immediately after hatching by their bright red eyes,

Facing page: Pied-factor Peach-faced Lovebirds: a Pied Green and a Pied Blue.

Left: Pied Dark-blue (Cobalt) Peach-faced Lovebird. **Below:** Dark-blue (Cobalt) Peach-faced Lovebirds can be distinguished from Blues by examining the rump feathers.

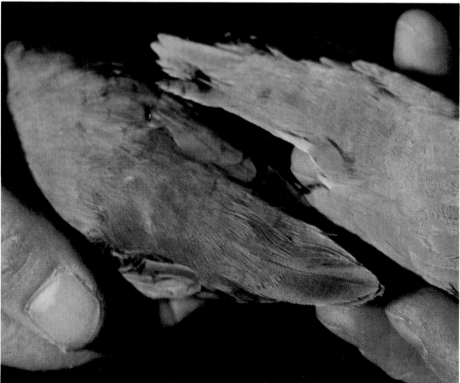

which retain their color even with increasing age. When fully colored, the Fallows have a yellow plumage, which is lightly tinged with green. The feet and bill are flesh color; the mask is a rich red; the rump is blue, but is lightened in comparison to the Green Peach-faced Lovebird. The eyes remain bright red. One can notice these red eyes even from some distance, in contrast to the eyes of Lutinos.

Fallow inherits recessively, as crossing results demonstrate.

The factor for Fallow makes the melanin granules in the barbs—that is, in the medulla—very small, and they are densely packed only in the middle of the cells. There are two different types of melanin, the black melanin, or eumelanin, and the brown melanin, or phaeomelanin. Though the two kinds of melanin differ in their chemical structure, they are nevertheless closely related, since one sometimes turns into the other. Thus one must assume that in Fallows only the brown melanin (phaeomelanin) is still present. It does not absorb as much light as the melanin in a Green bird. For this reason, here the blue structural color looks very weak, and the bird overall appears yellow with a green tinge. The black melanin in the eyes has disappeared completely, so they are red.

We wish to introduce the letter f for the factor Fallow; again we must not forget that the Green bird possesses factors for nonFallow, which we wish to represent with F, since this factor happens to be dominant. An inheritance diagram can then be quickly drawn:

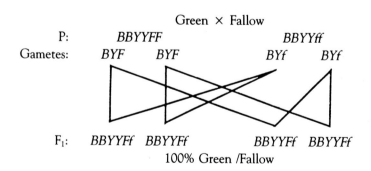

Green × Fallow

P:	BBYYFF			BBYYff	
Gametes:	BYF	BYF		BYf	BYf

| F$_1$: | BBYYFf | BBYYFf | | BBYYFf | BBYYFf |

100% Green /Fallow

The F$_1$ generation produces only birds that possess one factor for nonFallow and one factor for Fallow. These birds are therefore Green /Fallow. The backcross with a Fallow animal is shown below.

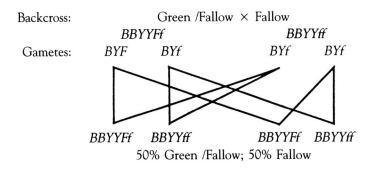

Backcross: Green /Fallow × Fallow

BBYYFf   *BBYYff*

Gametes: *BYF*   *BYf*   *BYf*   *BYf*

BBYYFf   *BBYYff*   *BBYYFf*   *BBYYff*

50% Green /Fallow; 50% Fallow

All Green birds from this mating are split for Fallow, and all others are, of course, Fallow. The interested breeder can very quickly calculate additional expectations on his own if he uses the diagram offered above.

Those few breeders who have this color variety in their stock at present should have maintaining and propagating them as their primary concern. This should take place with the greatest of care, and as many unrelated Green Peach-faced Lovebirds as possible, birds that conform to all the stipulations with respect to size and constitution, should be crossed in.

In the future, through pairings with other color varieties, new color combinations will certainly be obtained; for example, Blue (Pastel-blue) Fallows.

If one mates a Fallow with a Blue (*BBYYff* × *bbYYFF*), then one obtains in the F_1 generation young with the genotype *BbYYFf* only. These youngsters are all Green, but split for Blue and Fallow. Crossing this F_1 generation with each another produces, among others, 6.25% Blue Fallows (*bbYYff*). Further results can easily be calculated using the letter symbols introduced.

If we consider only the varieties which have been discussed so far, we can also expect the following birds: Pied Green Fallow, Pied Blue Fallow; Yellow Fallow, Pied Yellow Fallow, White Fallow, Pied White Fallow; Edged-yellow Fallow, Pied Edged-yellow Fallow, and Pied Edged-white Fallow. Indeed, even the combination of Yellow, Edged-yellow, and Fallow—as well as White, Edged-white, and Fallow—is conceivable, and both of these might also be combined with Pied.

This is a look into the future. Some breeders (see Ochs 1980) may well look forward to this trend with great apprehension, since thereby an eventuality, such as has already been experienced with the Budgerigar, can also be expected with the Peach-faced Lovebird. Many birds

The Green Cinnamon Peach-faced Lovebird displays the principal effect of the Cinnamon factor.

Facing page: Cobalt Cinnamon and Mauve Cinnamon Peach-faced Lovebirds.

Pied Cinnamon Peach-faced Lovebird. The presence of the Cinnamon factor is most apparent in the flight feathers.

will no longer be able to be classified correctly by phenotype. No matter how great the apprehension may be, that these birds will one day exist must be reckoned with, since the curiosity about what such animals would look like will induce many breeders to undertake pairings of this kind.

We have seen the Fallows produced in West Germany both in photographs and in the flesh; but we are acquainted with the Fallows of East Germany only through descriptions and from photographs. The birds from East Germany are much lighter than the Fallows in this country. They are very similar to Lutino Peach-faced Lovebirds, but, unlike them, they have bright red eyes and a light blue rump even as adults. We are of the opinion that these birds are one of the most beautiful varieties of the Peach-faced Lovebird.

At the present point in time, it appears certain to us that the Fallows from East Germany and those from West Germany are two different varieties. However, the Fallows from East Germany also exhibit recessive inheritance, like the Fallows in this country; thus the inheritance diagram we have provided can also be used for that variety. The question of what a cross of the two Fallow varieties would yield, will, of course, also occur to the interested breeder. This can be answered only once the two actually are crossed.

There is a possibility that the factors may be alleles (the gene, or factor, has then mutated twice). It is also possible that two completely separate factors are at work. Unfortunately, many obstacles stand in the way of an exchange of varieties, so that it will not be possible to answer this question in the foreseeable future, even though it is said that a few East German Fallows are already here in West Germany.

Olive and Dark-green Peach-faced Lovebirds. The time and place of origin of the Dark-factor mutation can no longer be traced accurately. The reason for this is that Dark-green Peach-faced Lovebirds have perhaps existed for quite some time but were not recognized (what Dark-green Peach-faced Lovebirds have to do with this mutation will be explained presently). In any case, the Olives arose from the Dark-green birds, which are said to have first been bred in Australia by Allan Hollingsworth (Hayward 1979).

As nestlings, Olive Peach-faced Lovebirds have a very dark, almost black bill. When fully colored, the birds look olive, as the name says. The flights are black, the rump too (perhaps becoming somewhat mauve gray), and the spots in the tail feathers are carmine red. The red mask is retained, and the feet and claws are dark.

From experimental crosses it is now known that the Olive Peach-faced Lovebird has two factors for dark coloration, or, as a breeder would say, two Dark factors. These factors apparently cause the walls of the cloudy cells to be very thin, so a large amount of light is absorbed by the melanin in the medulla, making the feather look darker. Thus, the olive is not itself a color, but again is a combination of the yellow of the cortex and the structural color from the interior of the feather.

We must assume that the birds possess the factors *BBYY*, and have additional factors for dark coloration, which we wish to represent with the letter *D*. Here too we must not forget that the green bird has factors for nonDark which we wish to represent by *d*. Therefore, an Olive Peach-faced Lovebird has the factors *BDBDYY*, and a Green the factors *BdBdYY*. If we cross two such birds, then we obtain the following inheritance diagram:

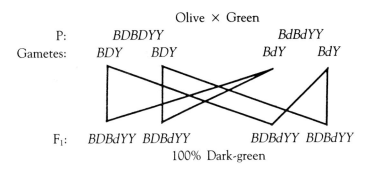

Olive × Green

P: *BDBDYY*   *BdBdYY*

Gametes: *BDY*   *BDY*   *BdY*   *BdY*

F₁: *BDBdYY* *BDBdYY*   *BDBdYY* *BDBdYY*

100% Dark-green

The birds in the F₁ generation all have the genotype *BDBdYY*. How do these birds look? They are the Dark-green Peach-faced Lovebirds already mentioned. In this case, one no longer has dominant-recessive inheritance (Ochs 1984), but so-called intermediate inheritance. The hybrids (with respect to this factor) have an appearance placed midway between the traits of the two homozygous parent birds, and are Dark-green. The coloration of these animals is a darker tint than that of the Green Peach-faced Lovebirds, from which they can be very definitely distinguished by the almost ultramarine rump. The plumage also appears somewhat duller overall.

If one pairs such birds with each other—that is, breeds to the F₂ generation—one obtains 25% Olive, 50% Dark-green and 50% Green.

The Blue Cinnamon Peach-faced Lovebird combines the Blue and the Cinnamon factors.

Facing page: The Cobalt White-mask Peach-faced Lovebird results from the addition of the Dark factor.

White-mask Peach-faced Lovebird. The presence of the White-mask factor is visible only in birds of the Blue series.

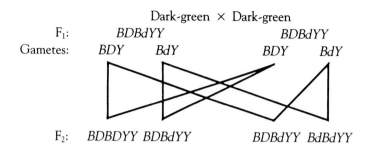

Dark-green × Dark-green
F₁: *BDBdYY* *BDBdYY*
Gametes: *BDY* *BdY* *BDY* *BdY*

F₂: *BDBDYY BDBdYY* *BDBdYY BdBdYY*

Dark-green × Green yields 50% Dark-green and 50% Green; Olive × Dark-green yields 50% Olive and 50% Dark-green. Thus, one can always tell unequivocally from the phenotype whether a Peach-faced Lovebird has inherited one or two Dark factors.

Mauve and Dark-blue Peach-faced Lovebirds. The idea of transferring these Dark factors to the Blues came soon, of course. At this point, we wish to make an exception; for once, we will not start with pure animals but, instead, consider the matter from a different side.

One can obtain Dark-green /Blue very easily, if one crosses Olives and Blues (100%), or if one pairs Dark-greens and Blues (50%). Theoretically, one would expect to obtain 25% each of Dark-green /Blue, Dark-blue (also called Cobalt), Green /Blue, and Blue from pairing Dark-green /Blue × Blue. But in our experience this does not seem to come about, and many breeders have also confirmed this.

Three pairs 1,0 Blue × 0,1 Dark-green /Blue produced, in a total of 17 broods, 70 youngsters for us. Of these young birds, 34 were Blue, 33 Dark-green /Blue, and 3 Dark-blue; Greens did not occur. Similar results were reported to us by other breeders.

To interpret this result, what was stated at the beginning of the section on wild-colored Peach-faced Lovebirds should again be recalled: the chromosomes are the carriers of the hereditary factors. Each species of animal, including the Peach-faced Lovebird, has a specific number of chromosome pairs. It is clear that not just one factor occupies one entire chromosome; since many pieces of genetic information are needed for the development of an animal, more factors than the number of chromosomes are present, in every case.

All of the inheritance diagrams illustrated so far began with the assumption that the factors (for example, *Y, B, P,* etc.) were on different chromosomes, so that independent assortment of these factors was possible (Mendel's third principle).

In this case, since the breeding results support it, we must take the premise that the factor for the formation of the yellow cortex (B) and the factor for dark coloration (D) lie on one and the same chromosome. This is called a linkage group. In the Green Peach-faced Lovebird, the factors for the yellow cortex (B) and nonDark coloration (d) also lie on the same chromosome. In a simplified sketch, it would look like this:

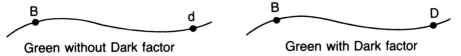

Green without Dark factor   Green with Dark factor

A Blue Peach-faced Lovebird also has a nonDark factor (d) as well factors for the lack of yellow in the cortex (b). In this case the chromosome would look like this:

The factors B and d, B and D, or b and d, are not separated from each other in the formation of the gametes. Being linked, they are transmitted to the offspring together, since, as a rule, the chromosome is passed on intact. For this reason, in the inheritance diagram for the Olive and for the Dark-green Peach-faced Lovebirds, we have paired the letters d and D with the Bs (we wish to continue this!).

It is apparent that the pairing Dark-green /Blue ($BDbd$) × Blue ($bdbd$) can yield only Dark-green /Blue and Blue birds. Why Dark-blues or even Greens are produced from time to time will be explained later.

Our initial pairing will be Olive × Blue.

$$\text{Olive} \times \text{Blue}$$

P: $BDBDYY$ $bdbdYY$
Gametes: BDY BDY bdY bdY

F_1: $BDbdYY$ $BDbdYY$ $BDbdYY$ $BDbdYY$
100% Dark-green /Blue Type I

In the F_1 generation, all of the young have one factor for yellow cortex (B), two factors for blue structural color (Y) and one factor for dark

Facing page: Wild-colored (Green) Masked Lovebirds, *A. p. personata.*

Left: Hybrid lovebird: Peach-faced × Masked. **Below:** Yellow and White Masked Lovebirds.

coloration (*D*), hence they are Dark-green /Blue. As the next step, we wish to examine the result of a cross between Dark-green /Blue and Blue. We should remember that *BD* and *bd* form a linkage group.

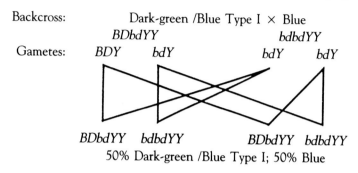

Backcross: Dark-green /Blue Type I × Blue
                    BDbdYY   *bdbdYY*
Gametes: *BDY*   *bdY*   *bdY*   *bdY*

    BDbdYY *bdbdYY*   *BDbdYY* *bdbdYY*
50% Dark-green /Blue Type I; 50% Blue

From this pairing, one obtains only Dark-green /Blue and Blue, since the Dark-green /Blue parent cannot produce gametes with the factors *bDY* or *BdY*.

Yet a small percentage of Dark-blues or Greens does occur. This is possible only if the linkage is broken. We now know that homologous chromosomes cling tightly together during the meiotic divisions. But in exceptional cases, pieces of the chromosome pairs can break off and join together again crosswise. In such a crossing over, all factors that lie on the separated pieces will be freed from their previous linkage group, and will be exchanged reciprocally. This event is called a crossover.

This can be shown in a simplified diagram, in which we have dispensed with the fact that each chromosome consists of two chromatids.

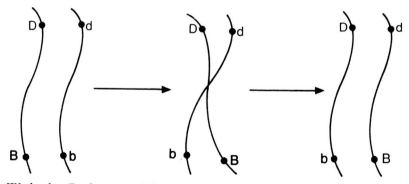

With the Dark-green /Blue, we have the linkage group *BD* on the chromosome which it received from one parent and the linkage group *bd* on the chromosome from the other parent. During the formation of the gametes, these two linkage groups can be undone and a new one formed; in this case, *bD* and *Bd*. Such breaks do not occur frequently, nor are they predictable.

If gametes with the new linkage groups *bD* and *Bd* on their chromosome have been formed in the Dark-green /Blue parent, then Green /Blue or Dark-blue youngsters could occasionally result from the above-mentioned pairing. These birds have these genotypes: Green /Blue: *bd-BdYY*; Dark-blue: *bDbdYY*.

Dark-green /Blues in which the Dark factor is linked with *B* are designated as Dark-green /Blue Type I in the Budgerigar, in view of the fact that one also can produce a Dark-green /Blue Type II (*bDBdYY*) when one pairs a Dark-blue Peach-faced Lovebird with a Green one:

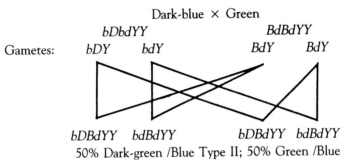

Dark-blue × Green

bDbdYY		BdBdYY	
Gametes: bDY   bdY   BdY   BdY

bDBdYY   bdBdYY   bDBdYY   bdBdYY
50% Dark-green /Blue Type II; 50% Green /Blue

From this cross, Dark-green /Blue young can also occur, but which have the linkage groups *bD* and *Bd* and therefore are genetically different from birds of Type I. If one crosses such animals with Blues, then, of course, virtually only Dark-blues (*bDbdYY*) and Greens (*BdBdYY*) result, unless crossover occurs again. Dark-green /Blues Type II can also result, for example, from the pairing Dark-green /Blue Type I × Dark-green /Blue Type I, provided a linkage break has occurred in one of the birds.

Therefore, the breeder must always consider that he could have two different types of Dark-green /Blues, which he would not, however, be able to distinguish by appearance. They can only be distinguished by the colors of their offspring.

The Dark-blues (also called Cobalts by some fanciers, in imitation of Budgerigars) have darker plumage than the well-known Blue (Pastel-blue) Peach-faced Lovebirds. They can, however, be clearly distinguished from the latter by their ultramarine rump. From such Dark-blues it is also relatively easy to breed Mauves as well. For this purpose, one crosses two Dark-blues with one another:

Wild-colored (Green)
Fischer's Lovebird,
A. p. fischeri.

Facing page: Blue
Masked Lovebirds.
One of the earliest
lovebird varieties to
occur, the
attractiveness of the
coloration has ensured
its popularity.

Black-cheeked
Lovebird, *A. p.
nigrigenis.*

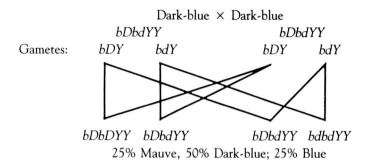

Dark-blue × Dark-blue

bDbdYY   *bDbdYY*

Gametes: *bDY   bdY   bDY   bdY*

bDbDYY   bDbdYY   bDbdYY   bdbdYY

25% Mauve, 50% Dark-blue; 25% Blue

Thus Mauves are Blues (Pastel-blues) with two Dark factors, and they can be clearly distinguished from other birds. Their coloration is very difficult to describe. Ochs (1980) describes them as birds which are lead gray on the upperparts and light gray on the underparts, where the gray has a reddish tinge. Other breeders describe them as purplish, which is certainly an exaggeration. This bird also, like the Olive Peach-faced Lovebird, has a mauve-colored rump; the mask is light reddish.

Of course, one can also breed Mauves from other pairings, but often these are due to an accident, since the linkage of factors must be kept in mind.

In breeding Peach-faced Lovebirds with Dark factors, one must be particularly careful that these birds do not become too small. Therefore, crossing in Greens or Blues is recommended in most cases.

Further Dark-factor Combinations. If the reader checks back, twenty-eight different varieties and possible color combinations (not counting the East German Fallows or the Dark-factor birds) have been described in this chapter. It is, of course, also possible to breed all these color varieties with one or two Dark factors. If one includes the previously described Dark-factor birds, this would amount to eighty-eight possible color combinations. Presentation of all these possibilities would certainly be beyond the scope of this book. One could, for example, breed Pied Olive Yellows, Pied Dark-blue Fallows, Pied Mauve Whites, or other combinations. Most of these birds do not exist yet, but they will certainly appear in the near future. At this point, we do not wish to make an assessment of such breeding endeavors but only to point to the considerations put forward in the section on Fallows. Some of these possible varieties or, more accurately, hybrid varieties, will no doubt be very attractive, more or less like some color combinations in the Budgerigar.

Unfortunately, we must forgo inheritance diagrams for these combinations, since there are hundreds of possibilities. The attentive reader can certainly draw them himself, using the previous examples.

Several of the varieties we proposed already exist, of course, notably the combination of Dark factors and Pied factors. Pied Dark-greens and also Pied Olives can be bred in one or two generations, respectively, as can Pied Dark-blues or Pied Mauves. We are of the opinion that the Pied Olives are especially pleasing, since the combination of olive and yellow, along with the red mask, looks very good to the eye.

Lutino Peach-faced Lovebirds. Lutinos first occurred in 1970 for Mabel Schertzer in San Diego, California. In our view, this is truly one of the most beautiful color varieties of the Peach-faced Lovebird. The birds have a brilliant, pure yellow color. The mask is a rich red, the legs are flesh color, and the claws light. The animals are distinguished from the other yellow varieties by their red eyes, which are clearly recognizable as such immediately after hatching. They also differ from all the varieties discussed thus far in their mode of inheritance, for this mutation is sex linked.

The reader will recall that in the section on the Green Peach-faced Lovebird, which attempted to present the fundamental processes of color inheritance, we stated that in the birds' somatic cells the chromosomes always occur in pairs (diploid). Yet there is something of an exception with the so-called sex chromosomes (gonosomes, or heterosomes). One pair of these chromosomes, found in the male Peach-faced Lovebird, consists of two that look similar, the so-called X chromosomes. In the female, the pair consists of one X and one Y chromosome, which differ markedly from one another in appearance. In addition, different factors lie on each of the females' sex chromosomes.

Sex is inherited in the Peach-faced Lovebird as follows:

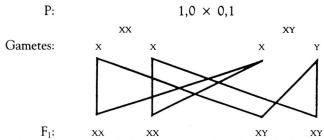

P: $1,0 \times 0,1$
                      XX   XY
Gametes: X   X   X   Y

F_1:   XX   XX   XY   XY

At the formation of the gametes, the diploid chromosome set is halved, as we know, so the gametes are haploid. Thus, from the male's

147

Yellow Fischer's Lovebird. Whether this variety occurred spontaneously or is the result of hybridization is uncertain.

Facing page: Wild-colored (Green) Fischer's Lovebird.

Nyasa Lovebird, *A. p. lilianae.*

gametocytes are formed sperm cells, which only possess an X chromsome (and the rest of the haploid chromosome set). The female, however, has gametes that contain either an X or a Y chromosome.

The union of the gametes at fertilization results in half of the progeny having the combination XX (male) and half being XY (female). The proportion of 1:1 males to females does in theory apply to our lovebirds, but in practice we usually obtain more females. The reason for this is probably that the males more frequently die in the egg or succumb as young, since they are more delicate, to some extent.

As we said, the factors, not all of which are known, that lie on the X and Y chromosomes are not homologous. However, we do now know that the so-called Ino factor, which causes a complete loss of melanin pigments, lies on the X chromosome. For this reason, only the yellow in the cortex is still present, so the bird is yellow. The eye color is red because here too all pigments are absent, and the blood in the eye shows through. With adult Lutinos, however, the red eyes are no longer as bright as in Fallows.

We again wish to introduce symbols, to be able to more closely examine the genetics involved. We will designate the Ino factor that lies on the X chromosome as i. Its allele is I, the factor for nonIno. We must also know that the factor for nonIno is always dominant to that for Ino. Therefore, a Lutino cock must have two factors for Ino; his genotype is *BBYYii*. If one crosses such a cock with a Green female (*BBYYI*ʏ) then one obtains the following result. (Since the Y chromosome does not carry the factors in question it is shown merely as ʏ.)

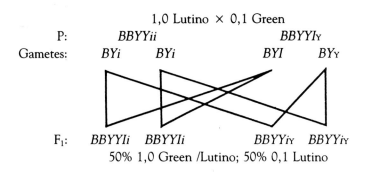

1,0 Lutino × 0,1 Green

P:	*BBYYii*		*BBYYI*ʏ	
Gametes:	*BYi*	*BYi*	*BYI*	*BY*ʏ

F₁: *BBYYIi* *BBYYIi*   *BBYYi*ʏ *BBYYi*ʏ
50% 1,0 Green /Lutino; 50% 0,1 Lutino

The 1,0 can form only gametes having i, but the 0,1 produce 50% with I and 50% without. It follows that all cocks that come from this mating are *Ii*. Since i is recessive to I, each young cock is Green /Lutino. On the other hand, the young females from this mating are all

Lutinos, since they have inherited *i* from the father and no homologous factor lies on the Y chromosome.

From this result, a general statement about sex-linked inheritance in the Peach-faced Lovebird can be derived: No hens can be split for Lutino! Cocks, on the other hand, can be heterozygous.

This pairing has a very great advantage: one can determine the sexes of the young in the nest, immediately after hatching. All Greens are cocks and definitely split for Lutino, and all Lutinos are hens.

Other expectations can easily be calculated if one uses our last diagram. It suffices to briefly list the results:

- 1,0 Lutino × 0,1 Green = 50% 1,0 Green /Lutino; 50% 0,1 Lutino
- 1,0 Green × 0,1 Lutino = 50% 1,0 Green /Lutino; 50% 0,1 Green
- 1,0 Green /Lutino × 0,1 Lutino = 25% 1,0 Lutino; 25% 1,0 Green /Lutino 25%; 0,1 Lutino; 25% 0,1 Green
- 1,0 Green /Lutino × 0,1 Green = 25% 1,0 Green /Lutino; 25% 1,0 Green; 25% 0,1 Lutino; 25% 0,1 Green
- 1,0 Lutino × 0,1 Lutino = 50% 1,0 Lutino; 50% 0,1 Lutino

Albino Peach-faced Lovebirds. The next step is to cross the Lutinos with the Blues (Pastel-blues) to obtain a new color combination, which is generally called Albino. The Ino factor, as was already mentioned above, causes all melanin to be eliminated, so that the blue structural color completely disappears. The birds developed in this way should be white and have red eyes. This is not the case, however, because the Blue birds are not truly blue, but pastel blue. The vestige of yellow (see the section on the Pied Blue Peach-faced Lovebird) is not lost. For this reason, the Albinos that we have today look cream colored; that is, they are tinged with yellow. The mask is rose, the feet and claws light. Some authors call them "Yellow-faced Albinos." We consider this appellation to be very confusing, since one cannot properly speak of a yellow face (see the section on the Pied Blue Peach-faced Lovebird); the name Pastel-albino would certainly be more appropriate (analogous to the internationally used Pastel-blue).

If one has Lutinos available, then one can very quickly breed Albinos. From the pairing 1,0 Lutino × 0,1 Blue one obtains the following result:

Wild-colored Red-faced Lovebird, *A. pullaria;* a male.

Facing page: Wild-colored (Green) Black-winged Lovebirds, *A. taranta,* male and female.

Wild-colored Grey-headed Lovebird, *A. cana;* a male.

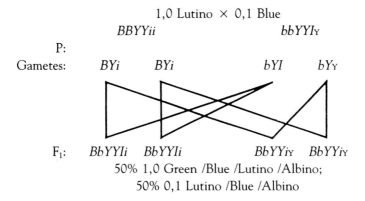

1,0 Lutino × 0,1 Blue

P:

Gametes:

F₁:
50% 1,0 Green /Blue /Lutino /Albino;
50% 0,1 Lutino /Blue /Albino

All of the young cocks are Green /Blue /Lutino /Albino, and all of the hens are Lutino /Blue /Albino. The heterozygosity for Albino results from the fact that Albinos are Peach-faced Lovebirds with the same genotype as the Blues, with the addition of the Ino factor. When one has such young birds, one can take several different routes to breed Albinos. Here is one of them:

0,1 Blue × 1,0 Green /Blue /Lutino /Albino

*bbYYI*ʏ *BbYYIi*

⊹

	BYI	*BYi*	*BYI*	*bYi*
bYI	*BbYYII*	*BbYYIi*	*BbYYII*	*bbYYIi*
*bY*ʏ	*BbYYI*ʏ	*BbYYi*ʏ	*BbYYI*ʏ	*bbYYi*ʏ

Thus birds with the genotype *bbYYi*ʏ result from this mating; these are Albino hens.

The other results correspond to those that were given for the inheritance of Blues and Lutinos.

Further Ino-factor Combinations. Since the Ino factor can be crossed into Blues as well as Greens, one can easily understand how the Ino factor can also be incorporated into all other varieties and combinations. Yet we seriously question whether this is worthwhile. The Ino factor is responsible for causing all of the blue structural color to disappear. Therefore, probably only a few combinations in which the crossed-in color will still be recognizable can be bred. Nevertheless, besides the Lutinos and Albinos, another eighty-six combinations, employing the previously described varieties and the Ino factor, are still conceivable.

A number of breeders have crossed in Dark factors, which are supposed to bring out somewhat richer color in the Lutinos. Usually this can only be noticed when Lutinos without Dark factors perch next to birds that do have them. Many fanciers believed, or still believe, that Albinos with Dark factors would be truly white. This is certainly a fallacy, since the Dark factors have no effect on the yellow remaining in the Albinos' feathers.

By crossing in the Pied factor, one occasionally obtains animals that have a smaller red mask (see the sections on Pieds).

Green Cinnamon Peach-faced Lovebirds. Cinnamons, a relatively new variety that originated in the United States, have captivated many breeders in West Germany. The name is taken from the bird's cinnamon-brown flight feathers. The green portions of its plumage are much lightened. The legs are flesh color, the claws light. One can easily recognize them in the nest by the wine-red color that glimmers in the eyes. This red eye color, however, can no longer be seen in older birds.

In structure, the feathers of the Cinnamons are much finer than those of Green birds. As a whole, however, the feather coat is very dense. Cinnamon, we suspect, is a mutation in which the black melanin is not produced, but the brown is instead.

The inheritance of Cinnamon is sex linked; that is, the factor lies on the X chromosome. Therefore, the mode of inheritance is the same as we have described for Lutino. For this reason, we will not supply another inheritance diagram, since one need only substitute c for i, not forgetting, of course, the C (factor for nonCinnamon) in place of nonIno.

With the Cinnamons too there can be only 1,0 Green Cinnamon, 1,0 Green /Cinnamon, or 0,1 Green Cinnamon; there are no heterozygous females!

- 1,0 Green Cinnamon × 0,1 Green = 50% 1,0 Green /Cinnamon; 50% 0,1 Green Cinnamon
- 1,0 Green × 0,1 Green Cinnamon = 50% 1,0 Green /Cinnamon; 50% 0,1 Green
- 1,0 Green /Cinnamon × 0,1 Green Cinnamon = 25% 1,0 Green Cinnamon; 25% 1,0 Green /Cinnamon; 25% 0,1 Green Cinnamon; 25% 0,1 Green

Wild-colored Black-collared Lovebird, *A. s. swinderniana*.

Facing page, above: Wild-colored Grey-headed Lovebird, *A. cana*, female. **Below:** Wild-colored Black-collared Lovebird, *A. s. swinderniana* (skin in the Senckenberg Museum, Frankfurt).

Wild-colored Black-collared Lovebird, *A. s. zenkeri*.

- 1,0 Green /Cinnamon × 0,1 Green = 25% 1,0 Green /Cinnamon; 25% 1,0 Green; 25% 0,1 Green Cinnamon; 25% 0,1 Green
- 1,0 Green Cinnamon × 0,1 Green Cinnamon = 50% 1,0 Green Cinnamon; 50% 0,1 Green Cinnamon

While we have treated Cinnamon as Green Cinnamon in this list of expectations, the Cinnamon factor can, of course, also be crossed into other varieties.

Blue Cinnamon Peach-faced Lovebirds. This combination already exists. Blue Cinnamons are very much lightened, with brownish flights, and have wine-red eyes when young. The mask is pink. Breeding Blue Cinnamons is not difficult: one crosses Blues into the Green Cinnamons. The second generation already yields Blue Cinnamons.

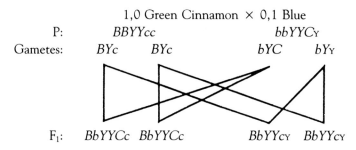

1,0 Green Cinnamon × 0,1 Blue

P:	*BBYYcc*		*bbYYC$_Y$*	
Gametes:	*BYc*	*BYc*	*bYC*	*bY$_Y$*

F$_1$: *BbYYCc* *BbYYCc*   *BbYYc$_Y$* *BbYYc$_Y$*

From this mating, only 1,0 Green /Blue /Cinnamon and 0,1 Green Cinnamon /Blue can occur.

If one crosses a male Green /Blue /Cinnamon with a Blue female, the following picture results:

0,1 Blue × 1,0 Green /Blue /Cinnamon

bbYYC$_Y$ ⚲	*BYC*	*BYc*	*bYC*	*bYc*
bYC	*BbYYCC*	*BbYYCc*	*bbYYCC*	*bbYYCc*
bY$_Y$	*BbYYC$_Y$*	*BbYYc$_Y$*	*bbYYC$_Y$*	*bbYYc$_Y$*

The young are 12.5% 1,0 Green /Blue /Cinnamon; 12.5% 1,0 Green /Blue; 12.5% 1,0 Blue /Cinnamon; 12.5% 1,0 Blue; 12.5% 0,1 Green Cinnamon /Blue; 12.5% 0,1 Green /Blue; 5% 0,1 Blue Cinnamon; 12.5% 0,1 Blue.

With the aid of the symbols, one can quickly calculate other expectations.

Further Cinnamon Combinations. Up to this point, there have been 176 possible color combinations that might be produced. One can, of course, also cross the Cinnamon factor into all of these, which would make 352 varieties. Many breeders will not be pleased with this development, but can it be halted? To the novice breeder of Peach-faced Lovebirds it may be said that while many of these combinations will certainly be bred, many will surely also disappear again, since their coloring will not be pleasing.

At present, the Dark-factor Cinnamons are very popular.

The attentive reader will certainly be able very quickly to calculate the results of particular pairings if he uses the symbols we've introduced. A few courses that yield Dark-factor Cinnamons will be mentioned briefly, however.

Initial pairing: 1,0 Green Cinnamon × 0,1 Olive = 50% 1,0 Dark-green /Cinnamon; 50% 0,1 Dark-green Cinnamon. The next step would be: 1,0 Dark-green /Cinnamon × 0,1 Dark-green Cinnamon = 6.25% 1,0 Olive /Cinnamon; 6.25% 1,0 Olive Cinnamon; 12.5% 1,0 Dark-green /Cinnamon; 12.5% 1,0 Dark-green Cinnamon; 6.25% 1,0 Green /Cinnamon; 6.25% 1,0 Green Cinnamon; 6.25% 0,1 Olive; 6.25% 0,1 Olive Cinnamon; 12.5% 0,1 Dark-green; 12.5% 0,1 Dark-green Cinnamon; 6.25% 0,1 Green; 6.25% 0,1 Green Cinnamon.

Since there are already enough Blues (Pastel-blues) with Dark factors (Cobalt and Mauve), Cobalt Cinnamon and Mauve Cinnamon are also very easy to achieve. In the expectations listed above, Green Cinnamon needs only be replaced with Blue Cinnamon, and Olive with Mauve; then, instead of factors for Green, Dark-green, and Olive, the offspring will be Blue, Cobalt, and Mauve, respectively.

To be sure, there are still many other conceivable pairings, not all of which can be carried out. The breeder should keep in mind that the Dark factor belongs to a linkage group (see the sections on the Dark-factor Peach-faced Lovebirds). From our own breeding, we know that Pied Cinnamons are also very attractive. Cinnamons in Edged-yellow and Edged-white (American Golden and Silver Cherries), which we have bred in recent years, also appeal to us very much.

Australian-cinnamon Peach-faced Lovebirds. In the first edition of this book (1981), we could report only the possibility that a second Cinnamon mutation existed in Australia. At that time, we were of the opinion that a combination of Cinnamon and Olive, or of Cinnamon and Yellow (Japanese Golden Cherry), was involved. Today we are

Wild-colored (Green) Peach-faced Lovebird in flight.

thoroughly convinced that it is a distinct mutation. Australian-cinnamons are very similar to Yellows (Japanese Golden Cherry); they are more yellow than American Cinnamons. Nevertheless, the flights show a light brownish color.

Australian-cinnamons are very different from the Yellows with respect to their inheritance, however, which is sex linked. Therefore, all of the tables and results from the section on the American Cinnamon can be used for this variety.

On the other hand, the pairing of Australian-cinnamons with Lutinos is very interesting. Dr. Erhart reported on this in the journal *Agapornis World* (1983). We have also received oral information from Herr Postema of Gieterveen (the Netherlands); on the occasion of a visit, we were able to evaluate his breeding results. He paired 1,0 Australian-cinnamon with 0,1 Lutino, and obtained 19 young birds from this mating. All were Australian-cinnamons, both cocks and hens! In reality, 50% 1,0 Green /Australian-cinnamon /Lutino and 50% Australian-cinnamon should have occurred!

There are two explanations; the first is this: The factor (gene) which is responsible for Lutino is also responsible for Australian-cinnamon; that is, the two factors are alleles. (Zebra Finch breeders are acquainted with this in Marmoset and Light-back, where a factor on the X chromosome has mutated twice.)

When we are dealing with alleles, then one factor must be dominant with respect to the other factor—in this case, the one for Australian-cinnamon. This is demonstrated by the pairing mentioned above, carried out by Herr Postema. We will again designate the factor for Lutino as i, and the factor for Australian-cinnamon as i^A. We will disregard all other factors.

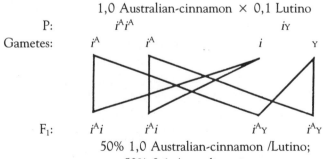

$$1,0 \text{ Australian-cinnamon} \times 0,1 \text{ Lutino}$$

P: $\quad i^A i^A \qquad\qquad\qquad\qquad iY$

Gametes: $\quad i^A \qquad i^A \qquad\qquad i \qquad Y$

F$_1$: $\quad i^A i \qquad i^A i \qquad\qquad i^A Y \qquad i^A Y$

50% 1,0 Australian-cinnamon /Lutino;
50% 0,1 Australian-cinnamon

All cocks among the young animals will have the genotype $i^A i$, and all hens are $i^A Y$. Since i^A is dominant over i, all the young must be Australian-cinnamons, with the cocks split for Lutino.

The pairing of 1,0 Lutino × 0,1 Australian-cinnamon should yield 50% 1,0 Australian-cinnamon /Lutino ($i^A i$) and 50% 0,1 Lutino (iʏ). This theoretically expected result has been confirmed for us by Herr Klompenhouwer of Winterswijk (the Netherlands), who carried out this pairing. The reports submitted from Great Britain (Cooper 1984) also support this explanation unequivocally.

Further expectations from pairings of Australian-cinnamons and Lutinos:

- 1,0 Green /Australian-cinnamon × 0,1 Australian-cinnamon = 25% each of 1,0 Australian-cinnamon /Lutino, 1,0 Green /Australian-cinnamon, 0,1 Green, and 0,1 Lutino
- 1,0 Australian-cinnamon /Lutino × 0,1 Lutino = 25% each of 1,0 Lutino, 1,0 Australian-cinnamon /Lutino, 0,1 Australian-cinnamon, and 0,1 Lutino
- 1,0 Australian-cinnamon /Lutino × 0,1 Australian-cinnamon = 25% each of 1,0 Australian-cinnamon, 1,0 Australian-cinnamon /Lutino, 0,1 Australian-cinnamon, and 0,1 Lutino
- 1,0 Australian-cinnamon /Lutino × 0,1 Green = 25% each of 1,0 Green /Lutino, 1,0 Green /Australian-cinnamon, 0,1 Australian-cinnamon, and 0,1 Lutino
- 1,0 Green /Australian-cinnamon × 0,1 Lutino = 25% each of 1,0 Green /Lutino, 1,0 Australian-cinnamon /Lutino, 0,1 Green, and 0,1 Australian-cinnamon

A number of breeders offer a different explanation of Australian-cinnamons, construing them as Lacewings, developed from American Cinnamons and Lutinos (Erhart 1984; also see the following section). We firmly believe that this possibility cannot be considered for the following reasons: There are Green Peach-faced Lovebird cocks that are split for Lutino and American Cinnamon. If one crosses one such cock with a Green hen, one obtains 25% each of 1,0 Green /Cinnamon, 1,0 Green /Lutino, 0,1 Cinnamon, and 0,1 Lutino. This result clearly shows that the factors on the X chromosome of the cock (c and i) cannot be alleles, since they do not affect one another. If they were alleles, than these cocks would have to be either Cinnamon or Lutino, depending on which allele was dominant over the other. In addition, the varieties that result from the pairing of 1,0 Lacewing × 0,1 Lutino are different from those coming from 1,0 Australian-cinnamon × 0,1 Lutino.

A great deal of confusion resulted when it became known that Australian-cinnamons were variably colored in their homeland. Today, we can explain this very easily: since there are very many Peach-faced

Lovebirds with Dark factors in Australia, these were crossed into the Cinnamons. Thus one finds there large numbers of Australian-cinnamons with one or two Dark factors, namely, Dark-green Australian-cinnamons and Olive Australian-cinnamons. The Dark-green Australian-cinnamons can be easily recognized by their cobalt-blue rumps, and the Olive Australian-cinnamons by their mauve-gray rumps. The flight feathers of the Olive Australian-cinnamons are darker, and the body feathers appear mustard colored. Thus these birds are also called Mustard in Australia.

The Blue (Pastel-blue) Australian-cinnamons still appear to be very rare in Australia; the reason for this is probably that our familar Blues (Pastel-blues) are still quite uncommon there. Since a sizable number of Australian-cinnamons are now in the hands of European breeders, it will not be long before new combinations with varieties already available appear.

Lacewing Peach-faced Lovebirds. By analogy with the Budgerigar, in Peach-faced Lovebirds the combination of Lutino and American-origin Cinnamon is called Lacewing. This name is certainly not appropriate, since the birds do not exhibit any lacy pattern on the wings, but it is now in use.

Dr. Erhart (1984) describes the birds as follows: dark red eyes; dark red mask; the yellow feathers are darker than in the Lutino and have a cinnamon suffusion; the large flight feathers are cinnamon colored. Unlike the Lutinos, Lacewings have blue rumps.

One cannot purposely breed Lacewings from Lutino and Cinnamon; on the contrary, they are an accidental result. It should be recalled that Lutinos as well as Cinnamons exhibit sex-linked inheritance and that the factors responsible lie on the X chromosome.

If one pairs, for example 1,0 Lutino × 0,1 Cinnamon, one obtains the following young: 50% each of 1,0 Green /Lutino /Cinnamon and 0,1 Lutino. From the pairing 1,0 Cinnamon × 0,1 Lutino, the outcome is 50% each of 1,0 Green /Lutino /Cinnamon and 0,1 Cinnamon. If one crosses the Green /Lutino /Cinnamon cocks obtained in this way with Lutino or Cinnamon hens, then one obtains the following results:

• 1,0 Green /Lutino /Cinnamon × 0,1 Cinnamon = 25% each of 1,0 Green /Lutino /Cinnamon, 1,0 Cinnamon, 0,1 Lutino, and 0,1 Cinnamon

- 1,0 Green /Lutino /Cinnamon × 0,1 Lutino = 25% each 1,0 Green /Lutino /Cinnamon, 1,0 Lutino, 0,1 Lutino, and 0,1 Cinnamon.

Thus combining Cinnamon and Lutino is not possible, as a rule, since the factors lie on different X chromosomes. Very rarely, however, crossover does occur (for a detailed description, see the section on Dark-factor Peach-faced Lovebirds). When this does take place, then the factors for both Lutino and Cinnamon are located on the same X chromosome and inherited as a linkage group.

For the Lacewing, therefore, we must use the symbol ic to represent the factors on the X chromosome. A Lacewing cock must always have the genotype $icic$, since the factor for Lutino as well as the factor for American-cinnamon must be present in duplicate, so that the bird is phenotypically a Lacewing. This significantly distinguishes this variety from the Australian-cinnamon. The pairing 1,0 Lacewing ($icic$) × 0,1 Lutino (iCY) produces 50% each 1,0 Lutino /Cinnamon ($iciC$) and 0,1 Lacewing (icY). From the pairing 1,0 Lacewing ($icic$) × 0,1 Cinnamon (IcY), 50% each 1,0 Cinnamon /Lutino ($icIc$) and 0,1 Lacewing (icY) occur. Of course, only young Lacewings would result from the Lacewing × Lacewing pairing. Additional expectations can easily be calculated with the aid of the appropriate inheritance diagrams.

Before long, the attempt was made to cross in Blues (Pastel-blues). This combination now exists. Dr. Erhart describes them as decidedly attractive birds; they are said to resemble Albinos, but with a weaker yellow plumage, dirty gray flights, and a light blue rump.

Lacewings have certainly existed for a number of years; but they were not recognized as a composite variety. As early as 1975, we saw an American-cinnamon cock, owned by the breeder Klompenhouwer, that passed on the Lutino factor and, therefore, must have had the genotype $icIc$. Combining Australian-cinnamon and Lutino to form a new Lacewing is not possible, since these varieties are produced by alleles. However, a composite of Australian and American Cinnamons as a result of crossing over is theoretically possible.

Australian-pied Peach-faced Lovebirds. For a long time, Australia has possessed another variety which probably also originated in that part of the world. Often called Australian-yellows, mature birds exhibit a deep, canary yellow color, occasionally with a green frosting. Moreover, some birds are covered with a greater or lesser number of light green spots. The mask is proportionally small and not as red as in the Lutino. The rump has a light blue color, or occasionally is a light green. The extent of the rump color can vary considerably but is never as great as on a wild-colored bird. In addition, the red band on the tail is usually absent, though now and then it persists in the form of a few red dots. The flights are white, the eyes black. The young frequently have even greener plumage, which, however, usually becomes more yellow with the molt.

Australian-pied inherits recessively. It is interesting, however, that heterozygous birds occasionally have yellow spots on the head or wings, and, in some cases, even have completely yellow head or leg feathers. These features are almost always lost with the molt, however. We hold the opinion, as do many other breeders (Roders 1983, Ochs 1984), that a recessive pied is involved in this variety, for the piebaldness is very pronounced. Since we must assume that the factor for Australian-pied is not an allele of any known mutated gene, we will introduce a new symbol for it: we designate the factor for the absence of Australian-pied as Q, and q for the presence of Australian-pied.

This may be clarified by several pairings:

- Green ($BBYYQQ$) × Australian-pied ($BBYYqq$) = 100% Green /Australian-pied ($BBYYQq$)
- Green /Australian-pied ($BBYYQq$) × Australian-pied ($BBYYqq$) = 50% each Green /Australian-pied ($BBYYQq$) and Australian-pied ($BBYYqq$)

Since a number of Australian-pieds are already present in Europe, it will certainly not be much longer before other composite varieties occur. It would certainly be interesting to combine the dominant Pied with the Australian-pied. Perhaps completely yellow birds with red masks and black eyes would result (see the section on Recessive-pieds). The procedure is simple: Pied Green (double factor: $BBYYPPQQ$) × Australian-pied ($BBYYppqq$) produces 100% Pied Green /Australian-pied ($BBYYPpQq$). These offspring must then be paired with Australian-pieds again; then one obtains, among others, young having the genotype $BBYYPpqq$; that is, Australian-pied with a single dominant-Pied factor.

In Australia, single and double Dark-factor Australian-pieds already exist. Very interesting too would be the combination of Australian-pied and Blue, so-called Australian-whites, which should show a very much lightened yellow.

Grey Peach-faced Lovebirds. Ochs (1980) mentioned that he had bred Grey Peach-faced Lovebirds. These birds have a dirty grayish blue plumage, with the underparts even lighter. The crosses that Ochs made permit us to suppose that Grey inherits dominantly over Blue. We have seen these birds but are not completely sure whether this is a matter of a distinct mutation or merely a variant of the Pastel-blue, which, after all, varies a great deal. We hope that further crosses will bring a conclusive explanation.

In a letter, Dr. Erhart reported that a variety is said to exist in the United States that actually does look gray. Unfortunately, we could not obtain further particulars at this time.

White-mask Peach-faced Lovebirds. About ten years ago, a new variety that had extremely distinctive markings appeared in Belgium. Today, it is universally designated as White-mask, even though the designation White-mask Pastel-blue would certainly be more appropriate, since White-masks only occur in the Pastel-blue series of Peach-faced Lovebird varieties. The upperparts of the White-mask in Pastel-blue are bluish green (with green preponderating), the underparts are light blue, the mask is white. A narrow red forehead band is occasionally retained, particularly by cocks.

About the inheritance of this variety there have been and still are manifold propositions. We believe, however, that the majority of them do not apply. On the basis of crosses we have conducted ourselves, and the interpretation of the results of other breeders, we wish to present this inheritance of this variety in detail.

It should be recalled that two factors are present for any inheritable character (if we except sex-linked inheritance for the moment).

A White-mask Peach-faced Lovebird in Pastel-blue must therefore have the following factors: two factors for the lack of yellow (bb), two factors for the blue structural color (YY), and two factors for White-mask (WW). A Pastel-blue Peach-faced Lovebird has these factors: two factors for the lack of yellow (bb), two factors for the blue structural color (YY), and two factors for nonWhite-mask (ww).

If one crosses White-mask with White-mask ($bbYYWW \times bbYYWW$) then all of the young must have the genotype $bbYYWW$ and must, therefore, be White-masks.

If one mates a White-mask Peach-faced Lovebird with a Pastel-blue bird ($bbYYWW \times bbYYww$), however, then the offspring are birds with the genotype $bbYYWw$. These birds of the F_1 generation presented great problems for breeders, since they are not White-masks (which would be the case, if the factor for White-mask were dominant over the factor for nonWhite-mask). Yet they are also not Pastel-blue (then White-mask would have to be recessive to nonWhite-mask). In fact, the offspring occupy an intermediate position with respect to coloration between the Blues (Pastel-blues) and the White-masks. They are tinged with green through and through, even though they are birds from the Blue series. Also, they have not a white but, instead, a rose-colored mask.

In Germany, because of the color, the name *Meergrün* ('seagreen') is given to these birds; in the Netherlands the designation is *Zeegroen*. Both are completely misleading conceptually, since one must not and cannot designate birds from the Blue series as "green"! For this reason, we have proposed (Brockmann 1983) to call these animals Seablues. Since, therefore, Seablue birds result from the mating of White-masked × Blue (Pastel-blue), it must clearly be a matter of intermediate, not recessive, inheritance, as Ochs (1984) maintains. We have already described the same mode of inheritance in connection with the Dark-factor Peach-faced Lovebirds.

According to the results introduced there, we can, therefore, say the following: Blue (Pastel-blue) has no White-mask factor. Seablue (Pastel Seablue) has one White-mask factor. White-mask (White-mask Pastel-blue) has two White-mask factors.

A similar case is known in the Budgerigar, in the so-called Yellow-face mutation, in which a Blue bird with only one factor for Yellow-face also shows it in the phenotype. But if these Budgerigars have two factors for Yellow-face, then the face is white! By analogy with the Budgerigar, one could, instead of Seablue, speak of a "Yellow-faced" Peach-faced Lovebird, but this would probably cause even more confusion among breeders.

In any case, we are quite certain that the White-mask corresponds to this Budgerigar mutation and not to the Pastel-blues (which are described as "Yellow-faced" in some publications).

If one crosses two Seablues with one another, then the result can be calculated very quickly: $bbYYWw × bbYYWw$ yields 25% $bbYYWW$, 50% $bbYYWw$, and 25% $bbYYww$—phenotypically, 25% White-mask, 50% Seablue, 25% Blue. Seablue ($bbYYWw$) × Blue ($bbYYww$) produces 50% each Seablue ($bbYYWw$) and Blue ($bbYYww$).

One question turns up again and again: Can one also notice the factor, or possibly two factors, for White-mask in the phenotype of a wild-colored (Green) Peach-faced Lovebird? Unequivocally the answer must be no. No bird from the Green series (that is, all birds that have *BB*

167

or *Bb* in their genotype—Green, Yellow, Edged-yellow, Lutino, Green Cinnamon, etc.) can exhibit a white mask, since it will not be visible because the yellow color in the feathers hides the factor or factors for White-mask! Yet Green-series birds that possess one or two factors for White-mask can occur, though one cannot detect this in the phenotype.

The following pairing might serve as an example: Green (*BBYYww*) × White-mask (*bbYYWW*) yields 100% *BbYYWw*, which is Green split for Blue and having one factor for White-mask; the bird is phenotypically Green. If one backcrosses a bird from the F_1 generation with a White-mask, then the following results: *BbYYWw* × *bbYYWW* yields 25% each of White-mask (*bbYYWW*); Green /Blue with two factors for White-mask which are not visible (*BbYYWW*); Seablue (*bbYYWw*); and Green /Blue with one White-mask factor which is also not visible (*BbYYWw*).

As far as we know today, no linkage occurs between the factors *Y* or *B* and the White-mask factor, nor is *W* an allele of *Y*. Therefore, Peach-faced Lovebirds which are phenotypically Green but have two factors for White-mask and are not split for Blue (*BBYYWW*) are conceivable. These birds look no different from normal Green birds, but they could provide a few surprises in breeding.

White-mask can be combined with all of the Peach-faced varieties in the Blue series—that is, those having the factors *bbYY, bbYy,* or *bbyy* in their genotypes. One can also breed very attractive blue birds by combining White-mask and Cobalt. Mauve White-masks are also very popular with some breeders.

If one has understood the inheritance of White-mask, then the procedure is not difficult: Mauve (*bDbDYYww*) × White-mask (*bdbdYYWW*) yields, in the F_1 generation, Cobalt Seablues (*bDbdYYWw*); these backcrossed with White-masks produce 25% each Cobalt White-mask (*bDbdYYWW*); Cobalt Seablue (*bDbdYYWw*); White-mask (*bdbdYYWW*); and Seablue (*bdbdYYWw*).

The combination with Blue Cinnamon is also easy to calculate: 1,0 Blue Cinnamon (*bbYYwwcc*) × 0,1 White-mask (*bbYYWWC_Y*) yields, in the F_1 generation, 50% each 1,0 Seablue /Cinnamon (*bbYYWwCc*) and 0,1 Seablue Cinnamon (*bbYYWwc_Y*). From 1,0 Seablue /Cinnamon (*bbYYWwCc*), through backcrossing with 0,1 White-mask (*bbYYWWC_Y*), one can obtain birds with the genotype *bbYYWWc_Y*, which are White-mask Cinnamon females.

Thus an almost unending series of combinations with White-mask is possible, especially because one can distinguish birds with one factor for White-mask from those with two.

Orange-head Peach-faced Lovebirds. Some years ago, Dr. Erhart reported to us that a new variety existed in the United States, which he called Orange-head, since a green bird did not display a red mask and head color but orange instead. This mutation is a recessive.

In the United States, many composite varieties—for example, Lutinos and Cinnamons with orange heads—already exist. We have not yet seen live specimens of this variety; the first Orange-heads are expected in Europe soon.

There is a hope that one could possibly develop truly blue animals using these birds, since these Peach-faced Lovebirds possibly lack the yellow pigment which is still present in the plumage of the Pastel-blues. This is yet another area of experimentation available to breeders in the future.

P. Frenger of Bedburg informed us that he produced a Peach-faced Lovebird in American-cinnamon that had a definitely orange head.

Violet Peach-faced Lovebirds. Dr. Burkard (1982) reported that in his breeding establishment a mating of Cobalt × Pied Blue produced a total of fourteen young, of which four Cobalts, one Blue, and one Pied Blue exhibited the Violet factor, although it was not detectable in the parents. He suspects that the Violet factor—as in the Budgerigar—is inherited dominantly.

Dr. Burkard describes the bird (Cobalt Violet) as follows: In comparison to the Cobalt it is distinguished by a significantly more intense blue color on the breast and belly, a darker back with stronger blue tint, and a cobalt-violet lower back.

Grey-winged Peach-faced Lovebirds. This variety is cited in several publications, and we have also received oral reports. We have not yet seen it, and we know nothing about the inheritance.

Red-eyed Pied Peach-faced Lovebirds. From the pairing of Lutino and Pied Green, in a few cases, Pieds with red eyes have occurred (orally, Wurche of Siegburg and Anschlag of Borken). Whether this is a matter of partial albinism or a new variety, as Ochs (1980) writes, we cannot judge. It is conceivable that the factor for Pied (which is actually a factor for partial albinism, that is, pigment deficiency), in some cases has spread to the eyes. We do not believe that this is a new mutation.

Red, Red-pied, or Red-edged Peach-faced Lovebirds. One occasionally hears of Peach-faced Lovebirds that have a red edging on some or on almost all body feathers. These are designated as Red, Red-pied, or Red-edged Peach-faced Lovebirds and are occasionally offered for sale in specialty journals. Certain breeders believed that they should ask astronomical sums for them. We are firmly of the opinion that no mutation is involved here, but only a modification (modifications are changes which are caused by particular environmental influences and are not inheritable).

For this reason, we (Brockmann) conducted a small experiment. Two animals, which could not be used for breeding, were for some time fed only plain canary seed; they received no supplements of vitamins, minerals, greens, etc. In addition, they were kept in artificially lighted quarters. After the next molt, the birds showed entirely red-edged plumage (Brockmann 1978, 1979). The two birds were then transferred to an outdoor flight and were given food that, we believe, met all requirements. After the next molt, both birds were again green. (After the publication of the results of the experiment, the procedure was labeled animal torture by some people. We do not wish to consider this point further, since we are of the opinion that the same sort of bird keeping, at least for our house pets, is the rule in many millions of households.) This experiment very clearly shows that the red edging must be a modification. Such red edging can occur in all species of birds with yellow color in the feather cortex. We cannot list the causes; many experiments would be required for this. This condition is certainly connected in some way or another with diet, however. Not only does the composition of the diet offered by the breeder play a role here, but, occasionally, so does the food preference of the bird, which, as is well known, does not always eat everything that is placed in front of it. Through improper feeding of the bird, or through incomplete assimilation of nutrients by the bird, changes in the construction of the feather could result, so that the psittacin is no longer absorbed by the keratin, but instead keratin is deposited as small kernels or clumps, which contain red psittacin.

We have encountered this phenomenon in many breeding establishments and with various parakeet and parrot species. For example: Green, Pied Green, and Lutino Peach-faced Lovebirds; Red-rumped

Parrot (*Psephotus haematonotus*); Red-fronted Parakeet (*Cyanoramphus novaezelandiae*); indeed, we have even seen a young Swift Parrot (*Lathamus discolor*), completely red, that died as a youngster.

In recent years, Lutino Peach-faced Lovebirds with red feather edging have won or taken high places at a number of exhibitions. We believe that such modifications do not belong at an exhibition, even when they are very attractive.

One can also observe such abnormal feather growth in Blue Peach-faced Lovebirds, only here the edging is not red but, instead, one sees light, almost transparent stripes.

In our opinion, the so-called Pink-suffused Golden Cherry, a Peach-faced Lovebird said to be a yellow bird tinged with pink, also belongs among the modifications. According to information by letter from Dr. Erhart (USA), this variant is said to be very popular in the United States, but it cannot be established by breeders.

Halfsider Peach-faced Lovebirds. As with the Budgerigar, a few cases of Halfsiders have already occurred in the Peach-faced Lovebird. These birds exhibit bilateral color variation (for example, blue and green). Asymmetrical color distributions can also occur. Thus, visiting Haverkotte of Ahaus, we saw a bird that was pied green on one side but had large areas of blue and olive on the other.

Halfsider is not an inheritable mutation! Halfsider females only hand down at most one color, even when they happen to be fertile. Halfsider males can possibly transmit both colors independently.

To our knowledge, no offspring of Halfsiders have yet been obtained in Peach-faced Lovebirds.

Prospects for the Future. We have attempted to detail the impetuous strides of recent years in breeding Peach-faced Lovebird varieties, and to present possible trends in the various sectors. We are fully aware that this development will continue in the coming years. This is not intended to suggest that only new color combinations will be bred, but also that many new mutations can still be expected.

The greatest wish of those who seriously pursue color breeding is that a truly blue variety will occur (with a colorless cortex). One could then breed pure white animals and true albinos, not to mention the other possibilities.

It is just as important, however, as has already been stated, that the different varieties and color combinations be given appropriate and universally accepted names. This is still a large arena for action by bird-breeders' associations, which should address this problem once and for all, so that designations, such as we in closing wish to quote from sales advertisements, will finally disappear: "Apple-green /Skyblue Green-winged (White-masked); Seagreen; White-blue Cream-winged Cherry; Apple-yellow Cherry; Dark-green /Seagreen Type I; Green /Skyblue Green-winged; Dark Seagreen; Purple."

Masked Lovebird, *A. p. personata*
Green Masked Lovebirds. The wild-colored Masked Lovebird was already described at the beginning of the book. The green ground color has the same composition in this bird as in the Green Peach-faced Lovebird.

Blue Masked Lovebirds. The first known Blue Masked Lovebird was captured in 1927 by the animal handler Chapman in Tanganyika (now Tanzania) and was brought from there to London. This clearly shows that color varieties can also occur in the wild. Blue Masked Lovebirds are truly blue, in contrast to the Pastel-blue Peach-faced Lovebirds. With them, all the yellow color has disappeared from the cortex and only the blue structural color has been retained.

The birds have a white breast, the bill is pink, the feet are gray. The areas of the plumage which are green in wild-colored birds are blue in this variety. This blue color is inherited in the same way as it is in the Blue Peach-faced Lovebird. In many cases, unfortunately, Blue birds are very small (as a result of inbreeding), so that crossing in large Green birds is highly recommended.

Yellow Masked Lovebirds. The yellow variety of the Masked Lovebird is said to have originated in Japan, but the time and the place are, unfortunately, not known to us for certain.

Yellow Masked Lovebirds are not truly yellow but instead exhibit a much lightened green in the plumage. The flights are whitish, the head has brownish frosting, and the bill is red. Such coloration shows that not all the pigmentation has been lost in Yellow birds; on the contrary, a substantial residue of melanin is still present. The inheritance of this Yellow factor corresponds to the Yellow variety in the Peach-faced Lovebird.

In Denmark, it is said that pure yellow Masked Lovebirds with red heads and black eyes have been bred. More details on this are, unfortunately, not known to us at this time. Based on information from Herr Jacobsen of Risskov (Denmark), it appears that a modification is involved in these birds, since they become greener with increasing age.

White Masked Lovebirds. With these animals, only the breast and neck band are actually white; the rest of the plumage is a dirty, washed-out grayish blue. This can easily be explained, for the White Masked Lovebirds are a combination of the Yellow and Blue varieties. Since the yellow has completely disappeared from the feather cortex in the Blue Masked Lovebird, it no longer appears in the White either. Therefore, the melanin that the Yellow bird still has can be seen clearly. One can breed White Masked Lovebirds in two generations from Blues and Yellows. The procedure is set out in the section on White Peach-faced Lovebirds.

Snow-white Masked Lovebirds with black eyes are said to have occurred in Denmark. Based on information from Herr Jacobsen, this too appears to be a question of a modification, since the birds, as they become older, have gray and blue feathers.

It should, however, be recalled once more that the following genotypes can occur in the Masked Lovebird: $BBYY$ = Green; $BbYY$ = Green /Blue; $BBYy$ = Green /Yellow; $BbYy$ = Green /Blue /Yellow /White (hereafter abbreviated to Green /White); $bbYY$ = Blue; $bbYy$ = Blue /White; $BByy$ = Yellow; $Bbyy$ = Yellow /White; $bbyy$ = White—where B = factor producing yellow in the cortex; b = factor for the absence of yellow from the cortex; Y = factor producing blue structural color; and y = factor for the absence of blue structural color (incomplete in the Masked Lovebird).

Thus there are no Blue /Yellow or Yellow /Blue birds, as one can, unfortunately, so often see listed in sales advertisements.

It is very easy to calculate that, if nine different genotypes exist, one has forty-five possible crosses. The crosses and their expectations are presented here:

1. Green × Green = 100% Green
2. Green × Green /Blue = 50% Green; 50% Green /Blue
3. Green × Green /Yellow = 50% Green; 50% Green /Yellow
4. Green × Green /White = 25% Green; 25% Green /Blue; 25% Green /Yellow; 25% Green /White
5. Green × Blue = 100% Green /Blue
6. Green × Blue /White = 50% Green /Blue; 50% Green /White
7. Green × Yellow = 100% Green /Yellow

8. Green × Yellow /White = 50% Green /Yellow; 50% Green /White

9. Green × White = 100% Green /White

10. Green /Blue × Green /Blue = 25% Green; 50% Green /Blue; 25% Blue

11. Green /Blue × Green /Yellow = 25% Green; 25% Green /Blue; 25% Green /Yellow; 25% Green /White

12. Green /Blue × Green /White = 12.5% Green; 25% Green /Blue; 12.5% Green /Yellow; 25% Green /White; 12.5% Blue; 12.5% Blue /White

13. Green /Blue × Blue = 50% Green /Blue; 50% Blue

14. Green /Blue × Blue /White = 25% Green /Blue; 25% Green /White; 25% Blue; 25% Blue /White

15. Green /Blue × Yellow = 50% Green /Yellow; 50% Green /White

16. Green /Blue × Yellow /White = 25% Green /Yellow; 50% Green /White; 25% Blue /White

17. Green /Blue × White = 50% Green /White; 50% Blue /White

18. Green /Yellow × Green /Yellow = 25% Green; 50% Green /Yellow; 25% Yellow

19. Green /Yellow × Green /White = 12.5% Green; 12.5% Green /Blue; 25% Green /Yellow; 25% Green /White; 12.5% Yellow; 12.5% Yellow /White

20. Green /Yellow × Blue = 50% Green /Blue; 50% Green /White

21. Green /Yellow × Blue /White = 25% Green /Blue; 50% Green /White; 25% Yellow /White

22. Green /Yellow × Yellow = 50% Green /Yellow; 50% Yellow

23. Green /Yellow × Yellow /White = 25% Green /Yellow; 25% Green /White; 25% Yellow; 25% Yellow /White

24. Green /Yellow × White = 50% Green /White; 50% Yellow /White

25. Green /White × Green /White = 6.25% Green; 12.5% Green /Blue; 12.5% Green /Yellow; 25% Green /White; 6.25% Blue; 12.5% Blue /White; 6.25% Yellow; 12.5% Yellow /White; 6.25% White

26. Green /White × Blue = 25% Green /Blue; 25% Green /White; 25% Blue; 25% Blue /White

27. Green /White × Blue /White = 12.5% Green /Blue; 25% Green /White; 12.5% Blue; 25% Blue /White; 12.5% Yellow /White; 12.5% White

28. Green /White × Yellow = 25% Green /Yellow; 25% Green /White; 25% Yellow; 25% Yellow /White
29. Green /White × Yellow /White = 12.5% Green /Yellow; 25% Green /White; 12.5% Blue /White; 12.5% Yellow; 25% Yellow /White; 12.5% White
30. Green /White × White = 25% Green /White; 25% Blue /White; 25% Yellow /White; 25% White
31. Blue × Blue = 100% Blue
32. Blue × Blue /White = 50% Blue; 50% Blue /White
33. Blue × Yellow = 100% Green /White
34. Blue × Yellow /White = 50% Green /White; 50% Blue /White
35. Blue × White = 100% Blue /White
36. Blue /White × Blue /White = 25% Blue; 50% Blue /White; 25% White
37. Blue /White × Yellow = 50% Green /White; 50% Yellow /White
38. Blue /White × Yellow /White = 25% Green /White; 25% Blue /White; 25% Yellow /White; 25% White
39. Blue /White × White = 50% Blue /White; 50% White
40. Yellow × Yellow = 100% Yellow
41. Yellow × Yellow /White = 50% Yellow; 50% Yellow /White
42. Yellow × White = 100% Yellow /White
43. Yellow /White × Yellow /White = 25% Yellow; 50% Yellow /White; 25% White
44. Yellow /White × White = 50% Yellow /White; 50% White
45. White × White = 100% White

From these possibilities, the breeder can select those that seem most suitable to him. Included are many matings that are certainly quite disadvantageous, because, for example, one cannot distinguish the four genotypes possible among the phenotypically Green birds. However, such crosses as, for example, Nos. 30 and 38 are very interesting, since one can immediately determine the genotypes of all of the young.

Pied Green Masked Lovebirds. Occasionally, one hears of Pied Green Masked Lovebirds. So far, however, we have seen only birds in which a few flights were yellow. We doubt a true mutation is involved in these animals. We believe that this is, in part, caused by abnormal feather growth and is therefore a modification.

True Pieds, about which we have received reports from Dutch and South African colleagues, have yellow spots scattered through the green areas of the plumage. The factor for Pied is said to be dominant.

Pied Blue Masked Lovebirds. The observations just made also apply to these birds. If one has a dominant-inheritance Pied Green Masked Lovebird, then one can, of course, cross in Blue animals and in the second generation obtain Pied Blue Masked Lovebirds (see Pied in the Peach-faced Lovebird). Crossing in Yellow and White Masked Lovebirds is also conceivable.

Cinnamon Masked Lovebirds. A number of years ago, Cinnamon Masked Lovebirds are said to have occurred in Japan, a few specimens of which are thought to have come to Europe. It is not known to us whether such birds even exist any longer. The inheritance is said to be sex linked (see Cinnamon in the Peach-faced Lovebird). Blue Cinnamons, designated Greys by other breeders (Hayward 1979), could result from a cross with Blue Masked Lovebirds. We could not find anything more specific about these birds either.

Grey-winged Masked Lovebirds. De Grahl (1973/74) reports the existence of a Grey-winged variety, about which, however, we could not ascertain any details.

Lutino and Albino Masked Lovebirds. These birds are hybrids of *A. p. lilianae*, *A. p. fischeri* and *A. p. personata*. They will be discussed in the chapter on the Nyasa Lovebird, since these were the foundation stock.

Dark-factor Masked Lovebirds. In 1983, at a lovebird exhibition held by the Parkieten Societeit in Luttikhuis (the Netherlands), we saw the first Masked Lovebirds with Dark factors (Brockmann 1983). This variety has been in existence for a number of years but only recently has it been in the hands of several breeders in Central Europe.

Dark-green, Olive, Cobalt, and Mauve Masked Lovebirds (for inheritance, see the Dark-factor Peach-faced Lovebird) already exist. The White Masked Lovebird with a single Dark factor in particular appealed to us. With the Whites, a considerable amount of the blue structural color can still be seen. With the Dark factor, the dirty blue of the White is replaced by a very rich cobalt blue.

Blue Masked Lovebirds with Red Bills. Dr. Erhart of the United States informed us of this variety. The photograph that was put at our disposal shows a Blue Masked Lovebird with a red bill, but a number of yellowish green feathers can still be seen in the plumage. This mutation is said to inherit recessively. By crossing in White Masked Lovebirds, one could certainly obtain White Masked Lovebirds with red bills in the F_2 generation.

Fallow Masked Lovebirds. Fallow Masked Lovebirds are said to have occurred in California.

Fischer's Lovebird, *A. p. fischeri*

Green Fischer's Lovebirds. The coloration of the Green Fischer's Lovebird has been described previously. The ground color has the same composition as that of the Peach-faced Lovebird.

Yellow Fischer's Lovebirds. According to de Grahl (1973/74), Yellow Fischer's Lovebirds were known in France as early as 1940. One yellow variety of the Fischer's Lovebird, now very rare, was brought to Europe from Japan. The bird's ground color is completely yellow, the bill is coral red, and the forehead is orange red. The mode of inheritance is the same as in the Yellow Peach-faced Lovebird.

These birds are so uncommon that only a few breeders in the world have been able to include them among their stock. This is undoubtedly due to the fact that the animals are certainly very delicate. Even in the pertinent specialty books, these birds are illustrated only in drawings or photographs which have been colored afterwards. Cultivating this variety and making it more robust by crossing in Green birds would certainly be worth striving for.

Nowadays, we somewhat more frequently encounter a different yellow color variety that more closely resembles the Yellow Masked Lovebird but which has a red head. Whether these birds are a true Fischer's Lovebird variety or are hybrids of Yellow Masked Lovebirds and Green Fischer's Lovebirds, we can no longer determine. Apparently, however, the latter is the case. These birds also follow the same mode of inheritance as the Yellow Peach-faced Lovebird.

Pied Green Fischer's Lovebirds. One also hears of this variety from time to time. In many cases, this certainly involves a modification, as was already described in the Masked Lovebird. From Dutch friends, however, we have heard that such a variety, which inherits dominantly, does in fact exist.

Blue Fischer's Lovebirds. De Grahl (1973/74) reports that a Blue Fischer's Lovebird, which has a whitish gray head, has appeared in California. Schwichtenberg (1982) also describes these blue birds, which are said to have originated in Czechoslovakia in 1964. Quite recently, news arrived from East Germany that this mutation has occurred in stocks there as well.

Already there are Blue Fischer's Lovebirds in the German Federal Republic and surrounding areas. We have seen several of these birds, and are of the opinion that these have, in part, come from hybrids of Blue Masked Lovebirds and Green Fischer's Lovebirds. We were even shown a White Fischer's Lovebird which we could clearly identify as a hybrid. Yet it cannot be disputed that a true Blue variety of Fischer's Lovebird probably exists. Unfortunately, we see a danger that, by crossing in Masked Lovebirds, the Blue Fischer's Lovebirds could be ruined.

Fallow Fischer's Lovebirds. Ochs (1984) reports that a Fallow once occurred in his stock.

Lutino and Albino Fischer's Lovebirds. These animals too stem from hybridization with the Nyasa Lovebirds.

Black-cheeked Lovebird, *A. p. nigrigenis*

No true mutations are known in these birds. Here too, a number of breeders are attempting to cross in Masked Lovebirds in various colors.

Nyasa Lovebird, *A. p. lilianae*

Green Nyasa Lovebirds. With these birds as well, the green ground color is composed of the yellow cortex and the blue structural color (see the Peach-faced Lovebird). Therefore, varieties similar to those described for the Peach-faced Lovebird are possible.

Blue Nyasa Lovebirds. According to Hayward (1979), there are Blue Nyasa Lovebirds. We could not determine if they actually exist. Their mode of inheritance would correspond to that of the Blue Peach-faced Lovebird.

Lutino Nyasa Lovebirds. The Lutino Nyasa Lovebirds are a very old variety, since they are said to have occurred as early as 1932/33 in Australia (de Grahl 1973/74). They have always been very rare in Europe, so that scarcely any breeder possesses such animals. In the United

States, on the other hand, a small stock of these attractive birds is said to exist.

The entire plumage is golden yellow, except that the head and the throat are a glowing orange red and the tail feathers and flights white. The bill likewise is orange red. This is a case of a bird in which all of the melanin—and therefore also the blue structural color—has disappeared (see the Lutino Peach-faced Lovebird). The unusual thing about these birds, however, is that the factor that causes the loss of the melanin is recessive. Therefore, males as well as females that are split for Lutino can occur.

A number of years ago, in the Netherlands, Lutino Nyasa Lovebirds were crossed with Masked and Fischer's lovebirds. Many generations of birds have been bred from these. Now designated as Lutino Masked Lovebirds or Lutino Fischer's Lovebirds, these birds are highly prized and correspondingly expensive. By crossing in White Masked Lovebirds, along with selective breeding, Albino Masked and Fischer's lovebirds have been produced.

The Lutinos are yellow and have a reddish head (the heritage of their Nyasa Lovebird and Fischer's Lovebird ancestry), and of course have red eyes. Albinos have white plumage and red eyes as well. These Lutinos and Albinos are certainly very attractive animals, but they are hybrids bred from Nyasa, Fischer's, and Masked lovebirds. This should be considered by all who wish to incorporate these animals into their stocks.

Hybrids Among the White-Orbital-Ring Lovebirds, *Agapornis personata*

As we have already established, all of the races of lovebirds with white orbital rings (Masked, Fischer's, Black-cheeked, and Nyasa lovebirds) are mutually fertile without limit. This fact could make pure white-orbital-ring lovebirds rare inhabitants of our aviaries in the foreseeable future. We wish to illustrate this with the example of the so-called Lutino and Albino Masked Lovebirds (see also the section on the Lutino Nyasa Lovebird).

The foundation stock for the Lutino and Albino Masked Lovebirds were male Lutino Nyasa Lovebirds and Masked Lovebird hens in various colors. Since the Lutino Nyasa Lovebirds inherit recessively, we must assume the genotype *BBYYii* for the homozygous bird. A Green Nyasa Lovebird would then have the factors *BBYYII*, in which *I* stands for nonIno and is dominant over *i*. A Green Masked Lovebird would, of course, also have the same factors, namely *BBYYII*. Since no linkages among these factors have been detected, we are dealing with three chromosome pairs in both cases. However, not only are the factors which have been introduced (*BYI* or *BYi*) present on these chromosome pairs, an enormous number of other factors are as well. If one crosses a Lutino Nyasa Lovebird with a Green Masked Lovebird (the factors of which are boldfaced, so that one can tell which come from which), then the following occurs: *BBYYii* × **BBYYII** = **BBYY**I*i*. Therefore, all offspring are Green and split for Lutino, and also heterozygous for all other traits that constitute a Masked or a Nyasa lovebird. Unfortunately, we still do not know the exact number of chromosomes in lovebirds, but we must assume that all lovebirds with white orbital rings have the same number of chromosomes; otherwise, the meiotic divisions (see the section on the wild-colored Peach-faced Lovebird) will not proceed smoothly, and unlimited fertility among the hybrids could not occur.

If one now crosses the hybrids of the F_1 generation with each other, 25% Lutino, 25% Green, and 50% Green /Lutino occur, but these exhibit considerable variation. If we examine only the Lutinos, then we can determine that the following genotypes are possible: 6.25% **BBYYii**, 6.25% **BB**YY*ii*, 6.25% BB**YY**ii, 6.25% *BBYYii*, 12.5% **BB**YY*ii*, 12.5% *BB***YY***ii*, 12.5% **B**BY**Y**ii, 12.5% *BBYYii*, and 25% *BBYYii*. Therefore, considering only two pairs of factors (*B*, **B**, *Y*, and **Y**), it must be surmised that 6.25% of the expected Lutinos are pure Nyasa Lovebirds (*BBYYii*), that is, 1.5625% of the total offspring. However, since these animals do have chromosomes besides those we have so far mentioned, the probability of purity becomes substantially smaller with each chromosome pair that enters into the question. With three chromosome pairs, it would already only be 0.14% (about one or two youngsters per thousand!). And with four pairs of chromosomes . . . Mathematically, it is completely unlikely that truly pure Nyasa Lovebirds would result from this offspring, since the animals have perhaps twenty, thirty, or even more chromosome pairs.

The attentive reader will not have failed to notice that birds with the genotype **BBYY**ii have also occurred, with many factors and chromosomes from the Masked Lovebird but unfortunately not all!

Even if one continues to cross in Masked Lovebirds for generations, the probability that all of the chromosomes, and thereby all of the factors, came from Masked Lovebirds is exactly zero, because, at the very least, the factors *ii* for the Ino factor (and thus also the chromosomes on which these factors lie) came from the Nyasa Lovebird.

Crossing over can be left out of our mathematical considerations, since it is likely that, through this process, factors from the Nyasa Lovebird will again be carried over to the chromosome complement of the Masked Lovebird.

Therefore, we must disagree with the opinion that truly pure Lutino and Albino strains of Masked or Fischer's lovebirds can be built up (Ochs 1982). They will always be hybrids.

With great pleasure we have ascertained that the large bird-breeder associations (for example, the AZ), have also espoused this view and no longer tolerate any Lutino or Albino Masked or Fischer's lovebirds at their exhibitions, since they are not the result of a distinct mutation.

The propagation of Lutino or Albino Masked Fischer's Lovebirds, however, has yet another aspect: If one breeds Lutino or Albino Masked or Fischer's lovebirds from Green and Blue, then in the Greens and Blues one can see, to a greater or lesser degree, that they are hybrids of Masked, Fischer's, and Nyasa lovebirds. Therefore, the breeder starts with Yellow and White Masked Lovebirds, which he crosses with the Lutino or Albino hybrids. All birds that result from this mating have again received the factors from the hybrids.

Many Yellows and Whites that result from this hybrid breeding are sold to other breeders as heterozygous birds, or as birds that are thought to be so. By crossing these birds into his stock, the fancier, in time, ruins his own pure stock (Brockmann 1984). If one goes through our bird exhibitions with open eyes for once, then one can certainly see among the Yellow Masked Lovebirds very attractive, and occasionally also pure, ones. However, the enormous color variation among the Yellows probably not only comes from selection, but is also a result of crossing in Fischer's and Nyasa lovebirds.

In recent years, the breeders of hybrids have set themselves a new goal: The Blue Fischer's Lovebird. For the reasons mentioned above, it is impossible to attain this goal, since the chromosomes that carry the factors for Blue in the Fischer's Lovebird still come from the Masked Lovebird. The calculation that, after fourteen generations, 99.21875% "Fischer's blood" is found in these birds (Ochs 1981) is erroneous. It is not "blood" that is inherited but factors instead; that is, factors on the chromosomes.

It must be conceded that one can scarcely distinguish certain hybrids (depending on how many factors—or, as the case may be, chromosomes—come from the Fischer's Lovebird) from true Blue Fischer's

Lovebirds. But the "by-products," and it is such animals that mostly are produced, are again crossed into Masked Lovebirds and so carry factors from the Fischer's Lovebird over to the Masked Lovebird. Almost no breeder would forgo selling these birds! And so long as enormous sums are offered for birds of this sort, one can hardly hold this against the breeders.

Can such hybrids be distinguished from genuinely pure varieties? This question is very difficult to answer, since it always depends on how many chromosomes—and therefore factors—from one or the other races are present in the hybrid. For example, we know breeders who have exhibited the same yellow bird one time as a Masked Lovebird and on another occasion as a Fischer's Lovebird. No judge took exception to this. We also know of such cases with Lutinos. One possibility, of course, always remains open to the responsible breeder: backcrossing with the wild form. If, from this mating, birds occur that do not resemble the wild type, then one can say that the mutant bird was a racial hybrid!

The hypothesis that from Blue Masked Lovebird × Blue Fischer's Lovebird, or from Yellow Masked Lovebird × Yellow Fischer's Lovebird, Greens alone must always occur (Ochs 1984) is one with which we cannot concur without qualification. Since both races, with a probability bordering on certainty, have the same chromosome number, the factors for the colors and their expression will also lie at the same locations on the chromosomes. So, if the respective corresponding factors should happen to be mutant, then only birds that show the mutated color can be expected from such matings.

The situation is different if it involves two different yellow mutations, such as the Yellow Fischer's Lovebird, which originated in 1940, and the Yellow Masked Lovebird known today. Since these birds have different phenotypes, it is almost certain that two completely different factors have mutated. As is known, of course, there are also different yellow mutations in the Peach-faced Lovebird. The mating of Yellow (Japanese Golden Cherry) × Edged-yellow (American Golden Cherry), for example, shows us this very clearly, since only Greens, heterozygous for both colors, result.

In this chapter we have only addressed a few aspects of hybrid breeding among the four races of lovebirds with white orbital rings. Upon serious consideration, an enormous range of possibilities reveals itself here. To ensure the preservation of pure lovebirds in captivity, all responsible breeders must exclude every one of the hybrids in their stocks from breeding! Only in this way can pure birds survive in our aviaries in the future. Already, there are entire stocks of Masked and also Fischer's lovebirds that must be designated as hybrids.

Here too one must compliment the large bird-breeders' associations. Despite the considerable efforts of certain breeders, Masked Lovebirds that have orange suffusion on the breast are assessed penalty points at the exhibitions. One should go a step farther: exclusion from exhibitions. To be sure, it appears that these birds are also found in the wild; however, it is not out of the question that there too hybridation with Fischer's Lovebirds has occurred (Brockmann 1984). In any case, a large number of these birds are produced by us through hybrid breeding.

And finally, a piece of well-intentioned advice for every breeder: that birds are imported does not mean that they come from the wild in Africa! They could also be birds that have been bred in captivity in any country in the world!

Black-winged Lovebird, *A. taranta*

Green Black-winged Lovebirds. Here too, the ground color of the plumage is composed of yellow and blue. Therefore, if one breeds these birds, mutations such as have already occurred in the Peach-faced Lovebird can be expected. But since these birds do not come into the hands of breeders in large numbers, and are bred only with difficulty, this is probably only wishful thinking.

Blue Black-winged Lovebirds. Hayward (1979) reports that a blue variety has occurred. No further details are known.

Cinnamon Black-winged Lovebirds. Vriends (1978) had a Cinnamon bird in his stock which apparently was wild-caught and imported in 1972. He describes it as a lightened green bird with some cinnamon-colored flights. The red of the mask was also lightened. Paired with a Green hen, this animal reared six young Green cocks.

Grey Black-winged Lovebirds. In 1982, a breeder advertised a Grey Black-winged Lovebird for sale in a periodical. Unfortunately, we could not learn any more details.

Grey-headed Lovebird, *A. cana*

No color varieties are known.

Black-collared Lovebird, *A. swinderniana*

No color varieties are known.

Red-faced Lovebird, *A. pullaria*

Blue Red-faced Lovebirds. Only the literature (Hayward 1979) suggests to us that Blue Red-faced Lovebirds, which inherit recessively, may exist.

Lutino Red-faced Lovebirds. In southern Europe a breeder has a Lutino Red-faced Lovebird in his stock. At this time, we cannot make any statements about the mode of inheritance.

A Request to the Reader

All the color mutations which are known in the Peach-faced Lovebird, and which we have discussed in detail, can, of course, also occur in the other lovebird species. Moreover, new varieties can also be expected in the Peach-faced Lovebird, even though the point in time and the nature of such mutations cannot be predicted. If new varieties should happen to occur, then we would be very grateful to our readers for any information. We will also accept comments and criticism with interest at any time.

Sincere thanks to all those who have written us in recent years, especially the members of the Arbeitsgemeinschaft Agaporniden (AGA, 'lovebird workshop'). — JÜRGEN BROCKMANN, Finkenstrasse 12, 4422 Ahaus 1, West Germany; WERNER LANTERMANN, Drostenkampstrasse 15, 4200 Oberhausen 13, West Germany.

Appendix: Color Factors
in the Peach-faced Lovebird

b = **Blue.** Autosomal recessive. Also Pastel Blue here and in Hayward's (1979) usage; called parBlue by Smith (1979). The African Lovebird Society (USA) has suggested that it be called Dutch Blue, and the name Marine has also been used. The normal allele is nonBlue, *B*.

W = **White-mask** Autosomal intermediate. The normal allele is non-White-mask, *w*.

y = **Yellow.** Autosomal recessive. Called parYellow by Smith, Japanese Dilute by Hayward. Japanese Yellow has been advocated by the African Lovebird Society. Also called Golden Cherry. The normal allele is nonYellow, *Y*. Varieties produced by combining this factor with the Blue factor were called parWhite, or Buttermilk, by Smith; Silver Cherry has also been used for this combination.

e = **Edged-yellow.** Autosomal recessive. Called American Dilute by Hayward; the African Lovebird Society has recommended American Yellow. American Golden Cherry has also been applied to birds exhibiting this factor. The normal allele is nonEdged-yellow, *E*. The combination of this factor with the Blue (*bbee*) has been called Dilute Pastel Blue by Hayward, American White by the African Lovebird Society; American Silver Cherry has also been used.

D = **Dark factor.** Autosomal intermediate. The factor was called Olive by Hayward and Smith, as were double-factor birds; single-factor birds were called Jade. The African Lovebird Society has proposed Medium Green for the single factor, Dark Green for the double factor, while Greens without dark factors would be designated Light Greens. Bielfeld's book (1981) employed the sequence Light Green, Dark Green, Olive Green. The normal allele is nonDark, *d*. In Blue-ground birds, the terms Cobalt (single-factor) and Mauve (double-factor) are common; double-factor birds have also been called Slate.

P = **Pied.** Autosomal dominant. The African Lovebird Society has recommended American Pied. The normal allele is nonPied, *p*.

r = **Recessive-pied.** Autosomal recessive. The normal allele is nonRecessive-pied, *R*.

q = **Australian-pied.** Autosomal recessive. The normal allele is non-Australian-pied, *Q*.

f = **Fallow.** Autosomal recessive. The normal allele is nonFallow, *F*.

i = **Ino.** Sex-linked recessive. The factor was called Lutino by Smith, and Hayward as well. The normal allele is nonIno, *I*. The Ino-and-Blue combination (*bbYYii*—Albino in this book and in Bielfeld's) has been called Cream Albino by Smith and Cream Lutino by Hayward, while the African Lovebird Society has suggested Dutch Blue Ino.

i^A = **Australian-cinnamon.** Sex-linked factor recessive to the allele nonIno, *I*, and dominant to the allele Ino, *i*.

c = **Cinnamon.** Sex-linked recessive. The normal allele is nonCinnamon, *C*. Varieties involving this factor have also been called Isabelle.

o = **Orange-head.** Autosomal recessive. The normal allele is nonOrange-head, *O*.

Bibliography

Aschenborn, C. 1954. *Bau und Einrichtung von Gartenvolieren.* Minden: A. Philler Verlag.

———. 1969. *Die Papageien.* Minden: A. Philler Verlag.

AZ/DKB 1968. *Einheitsstandard,* 4. Aufl.

Bates, H., and Busenbark, H. 1968. *Parrots and Related Birds.* Neptune, NJ: T.F.H. Publications.

Bielfeld, Horst. 1981. *Unzertrennliche—Agapornis.* Bomlitz: Horst Müller Verlag Walsrode. In English as *Handbook of Lovebirds* (T.F.H. Publications).

Boetticher, H. v. 1959. *Papageien.* Wittenberg: A. Ziemsen Verlag.

Bouet, G. 1961. Oiseaux de lAfrique tropicale, Teil II. *Faune Un. fr.,* 17/1961.

Brockmann, J. 1978a. Noch einmal 'Rote *Agap. roseicollis.' Zierflügel und Exoten* (DDR) 6/1978.

———. 1978b. Rotgescheckte Rosenköpfchen—Nichtwissen oder Betrug. *AZN* 7/1978.

———. 1979a. Niet weten of bedrog? *Parkieten Societeit (NL)* 1/1979.

———. 1979b. Rote *Agapornis roseicollis*-Rosenköpfchen. *Zierflügel und Exoten* (DDR) 5/1979.

———. 1981. Kreuzungsergebnisse der Farbmutationen beim Schwarzköpfchen. *AGA-Rundbriefe* 2–5/1981.

———. 1981, 1982. Vererbung der Farbmutationen beim Rosenköpfchen *(Agap. ros.). AGA-Rundbriefe* 7–12/1981, 13–17/1982.

———. 1982. Farbbezeichnungen der Roseicollis-Mutationen. *AGA-Rundbriefe* 15/1982.

———. 1983a. Eindrücke von der Agaporniden-Schau in Luttikhuis/Niederlande . . . *AGA-Rundbriefe* 33/1983.

———. 1983b. Nistmaterial für Grauköpfchen *(Agapornis cana). AGA-Rundbriefe* 34/1983.

———. 1983c. Rosenköpfchen-Weissmasken: Ein Beitrag zum Verständnis der Vererbung dieser Mutation. *AGA-Rundbriefe* 26–27/1983.

———. 1983d. Witmasker-Roseicollis. *Parkieten Societeit* 3/1983.

———. 1984a. Einige Gedanken zum wildfarbigen Schwarzköpfchen mit orangener Brust. *AGA-Rundbriefe* 42/1984.

———. 1984b. Vererbung der Lutino Schwarzköpfchen *(Agap. p. ?). AGA-Rundbriefe* 38/1984.

Burkard, R. 1973. Aus dem Farbkasten des Agapornis-Züchters. *Gef. Welt* 6/1973.

———. 1974. Zum Theme Farbmutationen bei den Agapornis. *AZN* 3/1974.

———. 1976. Zur Genetik des *Agapornis roseicollis. Gef. Welt* 4/1976.

———. 1982. Notizen aus meiner Voliere—Neur Mutation des *Agapornis roseicollis. AGA-Rundbrief* 17/1982.

Christ, M. 1983. Geglückte Zucht mit einem 0,1 Rosenköpfchen in Gelb (Japanisch Golden Cherry). *AGA-Rundbrief* 28/1983.

Cooper, N. D. 1984. Lutino and Australian Cinnamons Are Alleles of Each Other. *Parrot Society Magazine* 1/1984.

Delpy, K. H. 1976. *Grosssittiche und Papageien.* Minden: A. Philler Verlag.

———. 1983. *Agaporniden—Die Unzertrennlichen.* Minden: A. Philler Verlag.

Delpy, K. H., and Bischoff, S. 1982. Kaum bekannt: *Agapornis swinderniana. AZN* 7/1982.

Dilger, W. C. 1960. The comparative ethology of the African parrot genus *Agapornis. Zeitschrift für Tierpsychologie* 17, 6, 1960.

———. 1968. Studies in Agapornis. *Avicultural Magazine* 2/1968.

Duncker, H. 1929. *Vererbungslehre für Kleinvögelzüchter.* Leipzig.

Ebert, U. 1978. *Vogelkrankheiten.* Hannover: M. & H. Schaper.

Enejhelm, C. af 1957. *Das Buch vom Wellensittich.* Pfungstadt: Verlag G. Helene.

———. 1968. *Papageien.* Stuttgart: Franchksche Verlagshandlung.

Erhart, R. R. 1981, 1982. Zuchtbericht aus den USA. *AGA-Rundbriefe* 12/1981, 13/1982.

———. 1983. Notes from Europe. *Agapornis World,* 2/1983.

———. 1984. Lacewings Rosenköpfchen. *AGA-Rundbrief* 42/1984.

Forshaw, J. 1973. *Parrots of the World.* Neptune, NJ: T.F.H. Publications.

Franck, D., and Preis, H. J. 1974. Verhaltensentwicklung isoliert handaufgezogener Rosenköpfchen. *Zeitschrift für Tierpsychologie* 34/1974.

Frenger, P. 1983a. Die Vererbung der Dunkelfaktoren beim Rosenköpfchen. *AGA-Rundbrief* 25/1983.

———. 1983b. Zimter Rosenköpfchen *(Agapornis roseicollis). AGA-Rundbrief* 30/1983.

———. 1984. Dunkelfaktorige Zimter (Rosenköpfchen). *AGA-Rundbrief* 43/1984.

Grahl, W. de 1969. *Papageien in Haus und Garten.* Stuttgart: Eugen Ulmer Verlag. In English as *The Parrot Family.*

———. 1973, 1974. *Papageien underer Erde,* 2 Bde. Hamburg.

Hampe, H. 1957. *Die Unzertrennlichen.* Pfungstadt: Verlag G. Helene.

Hayward, J. 1979. *Lovebirds and their Colour Mutations.* Poole, Dorset: Blandford Press.

Kamer, R. u. B. v. d. 1981. Agapornis roseicollis *en zijn kleurmutaties in woord en beeld.* sHertogenbosch.

Kemna, A. 1976. *Die Krankheiten der Stubenvögel.* Minden: A. Philler Verlag.

Kronberger, A. 1976a. *Haltung von Vögeln.* Jena: VEB G. Fischer Verlag.

———. 1976b. *Krankheiten der Stubenvögel.* Jena: VEB G. Fischer Verlag.

Lantermann, W. 1978. Gerupfte Brut bei Schwarzköpfchen. *AZN* 7/1978.

———. 1979. Die Rosenköpfchen. *Die Voliere* 3/1979.

———. 1981. Unbefriedigende Schlupfergebnisse bei der Agapornidenzucht. *AGA-Rundbrief* 9/1981.

———. 1982. Zur systematischen Stellung von Agapornis personata. *AGA-Rundbrief* 18/1982.

———. 1984. Kritische Gedanken zum Ausstellungswesen. *AGA-Rundbrief* 43/1984.

Lehmann, O., and Seidel, P. 1980. Erstzuchtbericht *Agap. roseic.* Falb. *Ziergeflügel und Exoten* (DDR) 4/1980.

Loesch, W. 1977. Zucht der Agaporniden Gelber Fischeri, Erstzucht? *AZN* 11/1977.

Michaelis, H. J. 1974. *Der Wellensittich.* Wittenberg: A. Ziemsen Verlag.

BIBLIOGRAPHY

Moreau, R. 1948. Aspects of Evolution in the Parrot genus Agapornis. *Ibis* 90/1948.

Müller-Bierl, M. 1981. *Papageien haltung einzeln oder paarweise?* Minden: A. Philler Verlag.

Ochs, B. 1980. Roseicolliszucht: Entwicklung—Stand—Prognose. *AZN* 3/1980.

————. 1981a. Rein Gelbe und rein Weisse Personata mit schwarzen Augen. *AGA-Rundbrief* 5/1981.

————. 1981b. Die Zucht 'Blauer Fischeri' mit dem Ausgangs material Fischeri wildfarben x Personata Blau. *AGA-Rundbrief* 6–7/1981.

————. 1982a. Das Lutino und Albino-Schwarzköpfchen *(Agap. p. personata)*. *AGA-Rundbrief* 14/1982.

————. 1982b. Versuch einer Beurteilung der künftigen Aussichten der Agaporniden-zucht. *AGA-Rundbrief* 16/1982.

————. 1982c. Gelbe Fischeri. *AGA-Rundbrief* 24/1982.

————. 1983. Neue Mutation oder . . . *AGA-Rundbrief* 34/1983.

————. 1984a. Hat die Agapornidenfarbenzucht noch Zukunft? *AGA-Rundbrief* 40/1984.

————. 1984b. Die Mutationen des Rosenköpfchens. *Geflügel-Börse* 13–14/1984.

Pinter, H. 1979. *Handbuch der Papageienkunde.* Stuttgart: Franckhsche Verlagshandlung.

Prestwich, A. A. 1963. Breeding the Red-faced Lovebird *Agapornis pullaria*. *Avicultural Magazine* 1/1963.

Prin, J. u. G. 1983. *Les inseparables et leurs mutations.*

Radtke, G. A. 1971. *Die Farbschläge beim Wellensittich.* Minden: A. Philler Verlag.

————. 1981. *Unzertrennliche (Agaporniden).* Stuttgart: Franckhsche Verlagshandlung.

Reicherd, C. 1968. Etwas über Grauköpfchen. *Gef. Welt* 2/1968.

Roders, P. E. 1983. De Australische gele Roseicollis. *Parkieten Societeit* 5/1983.

Roders, P. E., and Brockmann, J. 1978. Kleurvererving bij Agaporniden. *Parkieten Societeit* 3–9/1978.

Schwichtenberg, H. 1982. *Die Unzertrennlichen,* 6. Auflage. Wittenberg: A. Ziemsen Verlag.

Smith, G. A. 1979. *Lovebirds and Related Parrots.* London: Paul Elek.

Soderberg, P. M. 1977. *All About Lovebirds.* Neptune, NJ: T.F.H. Publications.

Vit, R. 1975. Über Agapornis-Mutationen. *Gef. Welt* 2/1975.

Vriends, M. M. 1978. *Encyclopedia of Lovebirds.* Neptune, NJ: T.F.H. Publications.

Vriends, T. [M. M.] 1981. *Perzikkopdwergpapegaai (Agapornis roseicollis).* Best.

Wewezow, F. 1971a. Meine Erdbeerköpfchen. *Gef. Welt* 4/1971.

————. 1971b. Zucht der Erdbeerköpfchen. *Gef. Welt* 7/1971.

Wright, A. J. 1976a. Establishing Aviary-bred Madagascar Lovebirds. *Parrot Society Magazine* 1/1976.

————. 1976b. The Red-faced Lovebird. *Parrot Society Magazine* 4/1976.

Zürcher, E. 1977. Geglückte Zucht von Orangeköpfchen (veröffentlicht durch W. de Grahl). *AZN* 5/1977.

————. 1983. Neuerkentnisse über die Zucht von Orangeköpfchen. *AGA-Rundbrief* 27/1983.

Index